the machete mentality

The Fight for Your Future Self

The Machete Mentality

Copyright © 2022 by Robyn McLeod Thrasher

Robyn Thrasher Fitness, LLC

Robyn Thrasher Coaching

Printed in the United States of America

First Printed, 2022

Book Cover & Page Designs: Robyn McLeod Thrasher

Book Formatting & Layout: Owlsome Author Services

Editing: Owlsome Author Services

           Passardi Productions

           V.K. Withers

For information, please write to:

robyn@robynthrasher.com

You can also subscribe to the Author's weekly newsletter and blogs at:

www.robynthrasher.com

Please follow Robyn on Social Media platforms:

@robynthrashercoaching

ISBN: 9798840358375

A Book that Awakens You to

Surrender Your Old Self

Question Your Current Self

and

Fight for Your Future Self

alive

A Feeling of Everything

An Unapologetic Acceptance of Yourself

The Art of Appreciating Now

A Knowing of Your Soul

Samantha Jane & Dylan Hawk
Summer 2017

dedication

For My Children, Sam & Dylan

I Will Always Find a Way

to Make a Way

for You Both

I Love You Without End

non-negotiables

faith first

dream bigger

endure patiently

face your giants

live alive

never give up

do it again, but better

all the awesomeness **inside**

the machete **mentality**

Let's Fight

questioning

A Hunger for Knowing Yourself

An Opposition to Your Demons

The Art of Understanding Your Capabilities

A Knowing in the Need for Truth

is this book **for me**

have you ever dreamed so big and suddenly
found yourself standing on the edge of the
line of crossing into it BUT you just continue
to stand there watching it pass you by

Kind of an important question if you're standing in the store deciding and second guessing whether it's worth the price tag of investing your time and energy into reading the next 300 pages or so by someone you've never known, YET.

So, let's keep it quick and simple. This Book IS FOR YOU if:

You've been Settling.

You've been Suffering.

You've been sitting in Second-Best.

You've been Stuck.

You've been Struggling to get back up.

You've been Complacent.

And you've been Suppressing a desire to release the MORE inside of you.

THIS BOOK is FOR YOU if:

You have ever messed up.

Duh.

OR maybe you're caught in the middle of a mess right now.

It's for you IF you have ever lived a lie.

Maybe you're even suffocating in one today.

It's FOR YOU if you have ever been traumatized by your own insides. Repeating patterns and cycles you SWEAR you will stop staying stuck in, but refuse to get off the crazy train at the next closest pit stop, SO you find yourself going around and around and around, again and again and again.

This BOOK is FOR YOU if you have ever dreamed so big and suddenly found yourself standing on the edge of the line of crossing into it BUT you just continue to stand there watching it pass you by. It's roaring right there in front of you so loudly you can feel the vibration of it begging to be released and free. But YOU just can't seem to muster the step forward into it.

I have.

A few too many times.

So, this book is FOR YOU, if you're stuck and need a word to pull your ass up and out.

This book is for you if you need to start stepping up and FIGHTING for a future you know you CAN have but aren't sure how to get there OR if you even have the guts to follow through on something you can't see, but you can FEEL it tugging at you from the inside out.

Read on my friend.

This book is for YOU.

This book is going to be so tattered and dog-eared and highlighted and underlined on your nightstand table smiling at you to take him all in.

You want THAT life inside of you to be out of you. I know you do.

I get it.

I got you.

Keep reading.

Keep going.

I promise.

We're about to make a way through.

ROBYN MCLEOD THRASHER

hope

To Believe Anything is Possible

An Expectation Stronger than Fear

The Art of Holding on to Your Faith

A Knowing in Your Heart

my hope **for you**

to motivate, challenge, inspire and change some
aspect of your life that ignites a fierce fire inside
you like the one that burns inside of me

Inside these pages are my genuine Holy Spirit God given "hot damn, where did that come from," thoughts, feelings, curse words, notes and hopes for you and for me and for my kids and for my future life.

I am no therapist.

No counselor.

No legal anything.

I don't even do grammar right.

I write like I speak, and I PLACE my urge for you in the URGENCY of my content, NOT my lack of attention to proper periods, commas, apostrophes and some grade school oxford dictionary formalities.

I'm a rule breaker, bender and inventor of my own damn way.

And The Machete Mentality is just that. MY account of what works for me and what I've seen work over the course of my life as I strive for better. My life is still in progress. As is yours. If you choose IT to be.

These are my stories as I remember them in my head. Not yours. And, by any means, NOT "theirs" or whoever "they" may be. These are the memories I am exposing for you with great HOPE they help you. These are "my truths" as I lived them and continue to live WITH them every day.

And I am sharing them with you simply because this worked for me as I FOUGHT to find a way THROUGH when life kept happening to me and honestly, it pains me to think of leaving you behind.

So, this is me trying to pull you up, dig you out and take you on a journey with my roadmap that has helped me fight for my future self and walk with a relentless living for authenticity and an unstoppable awakening within my soul.

I encourage you to sit on the parts that strike a nerve, let them sink in and endure their truthful pain and FIGHT your subconscious attempting to block their blessings.

Let them question you.

Let them confront you.

Let them demand more from you.

Let them force you to face yourself as you are, right now, in this space.

My Mission here is simply to MOTIVATE, CHALLENGE, INSPIRE and CHANGE some aspect of your life that ignites a fierce fire inside you like the one that burns inside of me.

So, enjoy the pages. Apply what you can and START executing NOW. DON'T wait.

And by all means, my words are not mental health advice, legal advice, business advice or any other advice. I am an expert ONLY in my own experiences. As you ARE in yours.

This Book, This Roadmap - will lead you on a journey to help you get unstuck. To help you live the life God intends for you to live. Which I promise, is way BIGGER than you are even beginning to imagine.

Life is seriously not promised to you. And it doesn't wait for you to catch your breath. It keeps going and going and going and you have GOT to start building up the stamina to keep up. This Book will help you see that, feel that and start living in that.

My Purpose. My Passion. My Point. My HOPE for you reading this and soaking in its understanding is for YOU...

To Rediscover Your Hope

To Get up Faster When You Get Hit

To Find Faith in Yourself and in Your Dreams

To Look Within and Start Using What YOU Already Have

To Find Freedom from What Weighs You Down from the Inside Out

To Stop Settling in Your Own Messes

To Armor Up

To Rise Up

And to Learn to Live Alive Rather than Live in Your Lies.

freedom

A Place of Limitless Oxygen

An Abundance of Peace

The Art of Walking in Complete Surrender

A Knowing in Your Spirit

ROBYN MCLEOD THRASHER

cursing **caution**

digging yourself up and out of your own messes is
like drowning in the shallow end... and I bet you,
you can't do it without a few four-letter words

The power of a four-letter word can be striking.

I just used one in the previous paragraph, and you didn't even notice it, did you?

But you'll notice when I say fuck.

Gasp.

See?!

YET, you missed the more potent one.

L-I-E-S.

Lies.

AHH!!!!

Got you, didn't I?

Yes. I am smirking a little and you're just getting to know me. I will do this a lot as we go on this trip together.

BUT see... these four little letters, L-I-E-S, are more harmful than the Big F-U. That's my opinion at least. Yet we are so offended by the placement of four little letters that someone, somewhere, sometime long ago decided F-U-C-K was a "bad" word.

Yet we can lie and live lies and tell lies and breathe in our lies like a cancer and be ok with it?

Maybe I'm defending my need to still curse a little here because it's a work in progress I'm currently discussing daily with Jesus. BUT, until I get better at doing it less, Jesus says to come as you are. So here I am.

At the time I wrote this book, it was an all at war to dig out these dreams. It hurt like hell. It was a battle cry for a better life. So, four letter words were necessary for me to crawl my way up and out.

Digging yourself up and out of your own messes is like drowning in the shallow end. All you gotta do is stand up, yet the panic inside is more powerful than your ability to do so.

So, if you're offended by an f-bomb here and there (there really aren't that many), I invite you to challenge yourself and read it anyways, so YOU feel the power of the pain as YOU crawl your way out of an invisible scorching of the soul.

Mine.

Yours.

The one waiting for you.

AND the one dying for you.

You are either willing to bleed through some ugly to get to the gems of your life,

OR you are not.

It's your choice. And I've chosen mine.

But, I hope you decide to dig up with me.

And I bet you, you can't do it without a few four-letter words.

ROBYN MCLEOD THRASHER

dreaming

A Wonder of Everything that Could Be

An Ability to See the Unseen

The Art of Creating Reality

A Knowing in Your Soul of What Will Be

ROBYN MCLEOD THRASHER

it's just **a book**

we don't even notice the subtle sadness of putting
ourselves down when we're actually more badass
and brilliant than we give ourselves credit for

*N*ow, before this book was even published and public, I caught myself thinking negatively. I can still hear myself saying, It's just A Book.

NOW, Picture me as Joey from *Friends* using air quotes when I say, BUT it's not "THE BOOK."

It's messed up, right?

But we do this to ourselves all too often. Like blinking. We don't even notice the subtle sadness of putting ourselves down when we're actually more badass and brilliant than we give ourselves credit for. Instead, we belittle and downplay our own accomplishments.

So rather than judge myself for where I am not YET, but will eventually be, I would like to say, this is my first finished put on paper and in front of all eyes everywhere hold in your hand published BOOK. It's the first book I've let anyone read. It's the first book I have crossed the finish line screaming, Hell Yeah, I finally did it!

In Kevin Hart's hilarious laugh-out-loud-pee-your-pants-life lessons book,

The Decision, he encourages us to STOP and do just that. He reminds us to congratulate ourselves on small wins and big wins. To recognize our work. Our greatness. Our accomplishments. Our efforts. Our awesomeness. Because without acknowledgment, how will we ever know when we won?

I think we tend to fight with ourselves on that. We think it betrays our need to stay humble, calm and contain our ego, YET often the end result is US ignoring any good doing and succumb to shrinking ourselves rather than seeing ourselves succeeding higher than we ever think possible for us.

And while we do need to stay humble, there is a fairly thick line between being an arrogant bragging narcissist douchebag about it and simply stopping to smile at yourself in the mirror and saying Heck Yeah.

So, tap, tap on that back of yours.

I mean, seriously, when was the last time you said

Hell Yeah, I did it!

And WITHOUT a BUT at the end of it?

?

?

?

Think on that for a second.

Seriously, can you give me a win?

Oh wait, YOU did not KNOW this was going to be an interactive book?

Well, surprise!

It is.

So go ahead, I'll wait.

Do it right now.

.

.

.

Now, how good would it feel to say that out loud to yourself? To congratulate you on your wins. To remind yourself you not only got this, but YOU did this. You came through this. You lived this. You made this. Yes YOU. Amazing, brave, creative, resilient YOU.

So, let's start right off the bat by canceling out your Buts.

It's a four-letter word you don't need anymore, right along with all the lies you tell yourself.

I mean, seriously, how many of those bad boys do you flagrantly throw around every day?

I would do this but...

I did this, but...

I am going to try, but...

I went through this, but...

I overcame that, but...

I tried, but...

But.

But.

But Seriously!!!

Cut all your Buts.

They are sad and sappy and by the time you finish reading this book, we will have bleeped out all your explicit B-U-T-S from your vocabulary.

I've been working on this book for my entire career, but...

NOPE! Scratch that.

I've been working on this book for my entire career in my head, in my heart, in my mistakes, in my choices, even in all my delays. And surprisingly, I wrote the first draft in just 5 days and edited the second, third and fourth draft with endless loads of laundry being washed and folded in between, while shuffling kids to school and sports activities, taking client calls, filming videos for my coaching business and while tackling my inner demons who have tried to shut the door on me countless times.

I've been working on this book. This dream. This goal. This desire. And all these chapters as I struggled to live in my own adversities, screwups and life happens moments that feel like those old, hard back, bible-like Britannica encyclopedias that are too effing heavy to carry around with me one day longer.

I have been working on this book in every glimpse of my life being built by me, one choice at a time.

Through every success.

Through every struggle.

Through every coaching and training and mentoring and leading and teaching and owning a business and running a business and being run down by a business.

Through every client I've helped, let down and pissed off.

Through being a single mom of the two of the most amazing kick-ass kids you'll ever meet.

Through every heartache.

Through every tear filled with a grateful heart, as I witnessed God restore everything I messed up in my own brilliant way.

So, I think that does deserve a Kevin Hart pat on the back.

Since I was a little girl, all I ever really wanted to do was become a best-selling author and write books. She's been telling me to hurry the eff up for quite some time now because we've got six more to do.

So...

I HOPE I make you smile, laugh, cry, feel every emotion you've been ignoring, fighting, and lying your way through up until now.

I'm going to demand you to surrender your old self.

I'm going to force you to question your current self.

And I'm going to show you how to fight for your future self.

Because I can guarantee YOU - it's getting tired of waiting on you.

I HOPE I teach you in all my truth-telling-tough-loveness THAT you can do this.

That the pain you feel inside, whatever it might be, however hurting and heavy it is on your heart, it hurts way less to release it.

I know you feel like you should keep holding on to it

BUT.

DON'T.

DO.

THAT.

It's time to GET UP and STOP Giving Up.

You've Got This.

You've Got This.

Yes YOU.

YOU'VE Got This.

choices

To Make a Way

An Option for Opportunities or Obstacles

The Art of Going or Staying

A Knowing of You Becoming You

choose your **adventures**

**the power of getting to choose was too exhilarating
for my excited mind to wait and be still**

The fishhook caught my hand in that soft spot just between my thumb and pointer finger.

It happened so fast; I didn't have time to scream out a cry, a whimper or a curse word.

I felt a pull, looked down and it was just there.

Caught.

Hooked in my hand.

I was only eight years old at the time. Fishing with my family miles from nowhere. Standing there stunned and stuck when suddenly, I was jerked backward AGAIN as my brother yanked his fishing rod back towards the lake, unaware he had already taken hold of my hand. The hook, still attached to the line, lunged itself deeper in its new home.

My eight-year-old eyes widened in horror as I held my hand, stood shocked and blinded by the rusty barb sticking out of that sweet spot by my thumb.

We were miles away from anywhere in a time when cell phones didn't exist. There was no calling 911 and a doctor would be hours away driving on a two-lane winding, backwoods, mountain road.

My mom was freaking out.

My brothers might have been laughing ridiculously and obnoxiously hard.

But me and my second dad stood there contemplating and choosing our choices.

Option 1: Cut our day short, drive for hours to a hospital and wait to be seen by a medical professional (as medically as they get in rural North Carolina) and wither in pain the whole way there.

OR

Option 2: Take to his toolbox and see what he could do.

I wasn't crying. I was calm and not even thinking about what could go wrong. My mom had that all under control taking our molehill into a mountain of infection, surgery, losing my fingers, losing my thumb, losing my whole hand or the function of it, permanent nerve damage, even down to disfigurement. It was pure craziness.

But I was secure in his toolbox ability to assess and address my fishhook hand needs. After all, this is the same man I let pull a stubborn loose tooth from my mouth with a pair of needle-nose pliers just months prior.

That moment of choosing my choice was like living out my very own Choose Your Own Adventure Book. Remember those? They had two endings and you were supposed to choose this way or that way and turn ONLY to the page of your choice.

One Story.

Two Endings.

You Choose.

I always skipped ahead and read both options. The power of getting to choose was too exhilarating for my excited mind to wait and be still.

How often do we get to take a chance and choose like that?

To take a choice we've made and see which adventure takes you where?

To know in advance how it all ends. And if you don't like it, you get to go back and do it all over again.

That would be a fabulous way of living real life.

That day, both choices sucked for me.

Either way my hand would hurt.

But I could end the pain in minutes, possibly seconds, right then and there with my dad's skilled do-it-yourself plan.

Or

I could drag it out over miles and mountains and meltdown in the agony of awaiting its removal.

So, I sat down on a nearby picnic table and placed my hand on top. I watched and waited as he opened his toolbox and rummaged through metal handles and trays of this and that.

He explained his process of ending my pain.

I nodded and believed every word he said.

He cut the barb.

Careful not to leave a jagged edge.

Then he pushed it in and then in one quick tug, he pulled it out.

I don't remember screaming.

I don't remember pain.

I just remember as quickly as it had happened. I had CHOSEN for it to be over.

Choices are Ours.

Like the options or not.

You still get a choice.

It's a hard pill for some to swallow because it's easier to blame, point and disregard.

To suffer

To sit in it,

And to feel sorry for ourselves while we wait for the pat on the back that encourages the excusal of ourselves from our own lives.

I didn't ask for the fishhook that day.

But that's what I got.

Today, I am thankful for the scar that sunk into my skin. Back then, it simply represented an after the fact funny fishing trip accident that I held over my brother's head for years to come as most siblings do.

But now, the significance of that small scar still reminds me how my adventures are all up to me. And that my choices, well, they are a journey of self-awareness that make me or break me or accomplish both simultaneously.

The gift in it, regardless of the pain or pleasure, is YOU always get to choose, and those choices will take you one way or another, facing either a new set of obstacles or opportunities. Just like the fishhook in my hand.

Throughout this book, I'll ask you to choose. To make choices. To make decisions. To ask hard questions. To answer the even harder ones. You won't always like the proposal or the options at the end. But I promise if you're transparent with yourself – even if AND when it hurts to speak it out loud - the power waiting for you that comes from owning your way out is remarkably freeing.

So, what do I do?

I make ways through.

Let me tell you another story about me and my brothers to get us moving forward for your future you.

faith

To See Cleary, but Blindly

An Undoubted Belief in its Becoming

The Art of Certainty Without Proof

A Knowing in Your Gut

making **machetes**

the paths weren't just going to magically clear
themselves...we had to find a way to make the way

When we were kids, we grew up going to the Great Smokey Mountains every summer for the first two weeks of July.

Like clockwork.

We played for endless hours in the mountains and woods and forests and creeks and trees.

Except there were NO paths.

And there were NO trails.

Just endless shades of green and brown and weeds and plants and poison ivy our mom always warned us about.

There were snakes and bugs and flying insects bigger than my face. But we didn't care.

We were pioneers forging through the forests.

Seeking new land.

Searching for treasures.

Building forts and escaping the enemy.

It was bliss.

It was *Goonies* meets *Stand by Me*.

Now prior to all our forging – we had to find "machetes" to do all the necessary forging with. The paths weren't just going to magically clear themselves. We had to find a way to make the way.

Granted we were just 8, 9, 10, 11, 12 years old so we didn't get real machetes, but it was our job to find a big branch, pull off all the leaves, break the little twiggy branches and then transform it into a long stick. We then smoothed the long limb with a dull pocketknife we found hidden in my grandpa's shed. Our Mother took a blind eye, but I'm pretty sure she knew we were playing with grown-up no-no's and left it to God or chance that we didn't do more harm than good to our little warrior selves.

This smoothing of the twigs took hours. But once it was done, it was done and we had our machetes. We were weaponized and ready for any struggle that lived in the overgrown terrain that beckoned our names.

And for the next two weeks we could win the war and fight the fights with the flying big black cockroach looking beetle bug things that came out of nowhere buzzing in our ears, landing on our backs and getting stuck in our hair.

Armed with our makeshift machetes and childlike faith, we eagerly climbed the mountains.

Brave.

Fearless.

Naïve.

And Full of in the Moment Confidence.

The red clay stuck to our shoes and clothes and embedded itself deep in our fingernails. Only bars of Ivory soap would later scrub them clean. We had dirt and blood dripping down our elbows and legs from the scratches we gathered along the way as we swung our machetes and cleared our paths. Swatting the swords side-to-side and up and down. Sometimes we stayed in one place for a while just whacking

and whacking

and whacking

and whacking.

We hit the leaves and weeds and wild ferns mercilessly with our machetes.

We hit them up.

We hit them down.

We struck them side-to-side.

Whacking and whacking at the same spot.

Over and over

and over again.

The brush was thicker in some places along the way so we would just stand there whacking.

Incessantly.

Persistently.

Determined.

Believing.

Knowing.

We would eventually overcome the lush dense greens and clear a path to the unknown. Ultimately creating a new fortress in the world behind our grandparent's little white cabin.

The Ramsey Effect I called it.

Apparently, this find a way, nothing's going to stop us now mindset was in our blood stemming from my mom's father, "My PA." A man in my memory who fixed everything with grey tape and zip ties. A man who served his country, served his family, and served his career for a little past 75 years until his leg was taken from him from a blood clot or stroke or both. I can close my eyes, right now, and see the young age me staring at him standing in his front yard under a huge weeping willow tree with one cane, half a leg and a watering hose to feed the grass. He liked bacon grease on his popcorn and smoked a cherry flavored pipe, read the newspaper and always gave me the tightest, strongest two arm hugs. He was a simple man, yet his make it happen mindset worked miracles in my tiny little childhood hazel eyes.

He never complained to excuse himself from doing the job at hand. He had an answer for everything and was a man who never stopped for nothing coming on his tracks. He ALWAYS found a way.

The Ramsey Effect in me surfaces as Hardheaded, Stubborn, Determined, Forceful, Resourceful, Gritty, Tough, Powerful, Creative and most of all Hopeful. That when the day was too dark, my grandfather somehow always found a way to make it light. I inherited this trait as his blood, but its taking of me came in such a tenacious stronghold deep down inside that it bled into the roots of my core being, giving me the passionate perspective, I now call The Machete Mentality.

After hours of whacking our way through the unexplored land, our hands were calloused. Sometimes bleeding. And our little child arms were wet with sweat. Caked in dirt and clay.

Our clothes were filthy. Like jet black dirt mixed with that Carolina red clay kind of filthy.

Just filthy.

That's the exact word our mom would say.

Filthy.

You're both just so Filthy.

I can hear her saying it over and over and over again.

Filthy.

Filthy.

Filthy.

We would have to strip down at the doorway. Leaving the filth behind in the threshold of my grandparent's home. It was not welcome inside and would have to be washed away before we were allowed to enter for the evening. A bar of that bright white Ivory soap awaited us on a window ledge in a makeshift outdoor bathhouse/shed/mud room/laundry room my grandpa must have made at one point to appease many problems all at once.

How many times have you felt that way about where you are at in life? That you need to wash away the mistakes you've made. That you need a scrubbing of the filth you keep tracking back into your life. It's such a strong word, isn't it?

Filth.

So go ahead.

It's interactive time again.

Yay!

Seriously. I'm not kidding. Sit on it for a minute.

.

.

.

It's HEAVY, huh?

In spite of our filth, we kept forging forward anyways. We didn't care. Hell, we didn't even see it. We were so focused on making a path on fighting the invisible soldiers hiding out in our fields. We didn't worry about the weight of the filth that had found us. Stuck to us. Seeped into us.

We were out on the line forging new lands. New ways up the mountain side. And it was all ours for the taking. After all, we had created them. Macheted them. And we reveled in the mastery of that.

There was NO WAY we were going to be taken down, much less allow our woodsy fortress we had built with our own bare hands to be invaded or overcome.

So, we whacked and whacked and whacked some more. And we stayed out there in our fields forging all day. Up until dinner time and sometimes way past what was supposed to be bath time.

All day long, we had discovered creeks and water and rocks and rivers and made dams and looked for life in the wild that wasn't made of those big black beetle bug looking things.

We swung from tree branches to get away.

We swung without protection.

We swung with no helmets or padding to cushion and catch us when we fell.

And we fell.

42

A lot.

My second dad would yell at me,

Don't let go Robyn, as he watched me swinging from afar.

And you know what the first thing I did was?

Yep.

I let go.

Almost always.

Even then I had the keen ability to let go and feel that brief fleeting feeling that only comes in the exact millisecond moment from holding on so tightly to letting go and falling into your newfound freedom.

That ONLY comes from releasing into your own resilience.

And of course, the no nonsense approach to do exactly what I was told NOT to do.

I did that then.

I do that now.

And I don't plan on stopping.

Make a Way.

Machete that Shit.

Let nothing stand in your way.

That my friend, is The Machete Mentality I've come to live by long after my childhood machete whacking mountains days were over.

Making those makeshift swords, wandering in those woods and macheting our way into our own adventures is one of my best, most favorite childhood memories. I realize now it was seeding me for who and what I am today.

I'm the girl that makes things happen.

I'm the girl that keeps going.

I'm the girl that will break off a branch and transform it into a machete to find a way while a big beetle bug is buzzing in her hair.

I'm the girl that gets filthy.

Whacking

And

Whacking

And

Whacking

A

Way.

I'm the girl that doesn't let the filth, no matter how old or new or how deeply lodged into her pores it is, stop her from forging forward. I'm the girl that charges into uncharted uncertainty and lets go of the rope securing me safely.

I'm the girl that welcomes a dead-end road, rolls up her sleeves and waves everyone forward and safely ahead because I know no matter what I'll make a way through.

For me and for YOU.

What path in your life is blocked right now? Can you see a way through? Are you willing to step into the weeds and strike down whatever faces you in the unknown messiness waiting on the other side? Maybe you've done this in your past. Can you close your eyes and remember? Can you see the strong-willed child you used to be before the filth took on too many layers? Will you choose to make your machete and start swinging at anything standing in your way? Emotions. Feelings. Fear. Situations. Struggles. Or will you choose to stay on the outskirts of the possibilities beyond the tall weeds and the big black beetle bugs?

Choose your adventure or choose your adversity. Honestly, they are about the same.

relentless

A Never Give Up Tenacity

An Attitude that Finds a Way

The Art of Enduring Patiently

and Urgently Simultaneously

A Knowing in Knowing Eventually

Will Come Through for You

that's why i got you

he was witnessing my faith in the making
of a dream come to life

Sitting at the bar with my love, sipping on red wine and splitting a pretzel, my boyfriend told me that's why he got me.

Wait, what? I asked cocking my head to the side.

That's why I got you.

That's why you what?

That's why I got you. He said smiling, catching my eye with his effortless wink, while his hand gently patted my knee.

We had been talking about my coaching business and recent overnight success that was seven years in the making after opening my brick-and-mortar gym.

Because YOU make a way.

You make things happen. That's why I got you, he said.

He could have repeated it ten more times. You can insert a big ole smiley heart-eyed emoji here and plant it on my googly-eyed face. I gazed back at him with an admiration and a love that went way past the moon and back.

What he said to me was a better compliment than him saying you looked beautiful tonight. That my fishhook in hand, tooth-pulling, mountain climbing machete swinging 8-year-old self, made shit happen then and is making shit happen now.

It was music to my ears.

His recognition of that confirmed for me that what I'd been sowing in the dark for what seemed like an endless eternity was finally breaking light.

He could see what I could see in my head.

He was witnessing my faith in the making of a dream come to life.

That after 26 years of wrapping my identity up in pull-ups and pushups and picking up weights to the pulsating beat of hip hop, gangster rap, dance, 80s rock, and yes, even Christian music too – I had finally detached myself from what I do physically, from what I've always done to pay the bills and had FINALLY begun anchoring myself to who I was becoming.

A child of God.

A woman empowering others.

A mother on a mission.

A little girl living her dream.

A human just trying to help people see possibilities in spite of their pain and problems.

A nobody trying to realize SHE IS already somebody.

Like the fishing line linked to the hook in my hand, I was just now finding my own freedom beyond the high-fiving fitness training that I had tenaciously been clinging to. Even though the water was well above my head, I was just too stubborn to stand up and walk out of the shallow end of it. I was drowning in my own puddle. Way in over my head, trying to keep up the exorbitant expenses of a fancy brick building, 17-hour days, alone and lost and lingering far too long in a place I had outgrown.

YET, God had me right where he wanted me all along. Hiding in the atta boys and pats on the back and snuck in between all my tough love and just-one-more-rep coaching commands, He had already been helping me help people from the inside out in a chameleon like way - through all my crazy exercises there had been an under the radar exorcism of their old lifeless life taking place. It had ALWAYS been about MORE than just fitness. I just didn't know it then, but I revel in the wonderment of it now.

My Machete Mentality to drive out their demons defeating them down was right there all along. My ministry for fighting for an unsettling life was hiding in plain sight underneath all the heaviness in their hope they hoarded in their hearts.

And it was my job to pull it out and expose it.

The answers were always within me, as they are you. They are disguised by overthinking, procrastination, unworthiness, inept, ill-equipped, super insecure yet amazingly, and somehow still confidently craving that aha-life-changing-brilliant-badass moment that validates all the crazy ideas, all the long cries and all the lonely gaps in-between knowing...

I mean KNOWING, truly, undeniably, undoubtedly, KNOWING that the two lives we live... simply CANNOT co-exist.

We must FIGHT for one or the other.

But NOT for both.

I am here to help you fight the right fight. Lucky for you, you already have everything you need inside. It's just a matter of choosing the life you are living or the one trapped inside.

What fight are you in right now? The fight for your old self? Your used to be self? The once was self? Or are you fighting for your future self? Your becoming? Your legacy? Your Moment right now self?

decide

A Choice to Act Courageously

An Effort to Take on Adventures

The Art of Living Actively

A Knowing in the Authority of Your Choices

choosing **choices**

that kind of alive is the jaw dropping sunset seeing
breath-taking ocean walking waves crashing on the
cliff's beauty ONLY God's love and triumph can inspire

Spoiler Alert.

If you haven't figured it out by now, I think and believe and breathe by CHOICES.

I help people see that. They don't always like it or receive it or accept it or perceive it that way. But that's what I'm doing. That's my intention.

It is the backbone of my belief system. To get the life you want. You must make choices constantly and consistently and re-commit daily, sometimes hourly, to the life you want OR you will get stuck in the one you don't. It's a choosing to stop feeding the life feeding on you and feed the one that fuels you.

My mission is to help people feed the right life. The one they wish existed. The one they don't need a break from. To stop settling. To transition and move through adversity rather than get sucked in by it. And ultimately, to rise into their resiliency. To get up faster and stronger and with less filth attached along the way.

I help people create courage to stop giving up on themselves. To stand on their own.

To come out of hiding and to Live Alive. Like, to actually wake up loving what they get to do today, loving who they are today, loving their perfectly imperfect life.

That kind of alive is the jaw dropping sunset seeing breath-taking ocean walking waves crashing on the cliff's beauty ONLY God's love and triumph can inspire. That kind of speechless peace is the freedom I'm determined to help people discover.

Freedom from their invisible insecurities and external excuses. You know, those things that keep us anchored to an old, outdated, used up version of ourselves. Illusions of what once was, but no longer is and never will be again. Shattering those old stories shrinking us, shrinking you, shrinking even me. That's the mission.

And then, CREATING a life they love. You love. I love.

Building that new life, in the midst of surrendering the old life. Growing into the life you keep saying you are dying to live YET are still STUCK sucking up all the oxygen for the old one.

Still STUCK living with that deep down inside invisible every damn day pain. SETTLED securely in your struggles – fully engaged in an all-out ceaseless game of tug-of-war from what is and what was and what should have been - TO actually MOVING forward and taking hold of what is waiting for you.

There is a war waging within.

Choosing choices that correct you is painful.

Choosing choices that change you is painful.

But choosing choices that keep shrinking you is NO choice at all.

It's a death sentence for your future self.

I want to help YOU fill the gap in between all the pain and sadness with God and His goodness. I want to help YOU fulfill your gifts and talents and calling and purpose and passions and adventures that He wants for us. I want to help YOU live IN your LEGACY rather than just leave it behind for others to quote and live half-ass inspired by. I want to help GIVE you permission to live UNRELENTING in welcoming YOUR dream life into this here right now life.

Not a settling.

Not a surviving.

Not a content and especially not a comfortable easy way-out life.

But rather, a living out loud life. A coming off the back burner life. A raising your hand first life. A deliberate hungry life. A jumping in when everyone else is just pacing back and forth talking about how beautiful it is life.

AND I help people experience that by exposing all my MESSED up wrong turns in life that have ultimately created my perfectly imperfect love my life-LIFE.

Make no mistake.

This IS a relentless pursuit.

With an enduring patience.

With an expectation of victory.

With a faith that IT, whatever it is for you, has already happened.

With the choice to choose resilience and authenticity and an authority in who you are NOW and who you are becoming.

It's a choice to live without all the lies, to make the machete, to forge forward and to carve out the life waiting for YOU beyond all the weeds.

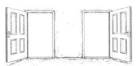

What is the life inside you asking you to do? What's the thing that's not going away? What's the tugging inside telling you? When are you going to answer it? How much longer must it beg for you to believe in it? Hasn't it waited long enough? What are you waiting for anyway? The weeds are just going to get thicker, and the beetle bugs will only get bigger.

suffer

A Choice to Bleed Unnecessarily

An Excuse to Stop Living

The Art of Doing Nothing with Pain

A Knowing of Giving Up

getting back **in line**

they had made their machetes and came in
hot swinging left and right

Now, all that might sound arrogantly ambitious. You're thinking maybe she got carried away with the whole Kevin Hart personal atta boy thing. But just keep reading. It so isn't.

I've written this book to give you some light to finding your freedom. A roadmap for relentless resilience. Honestly, it's not rocket science. I am NOT that smart. But what I am, is HUNGRY. And Brave. And Bold. And in a relentless pursuit to help YOU find your FREEDOM, as I have found mine.

There is nothing in here you probably haven't read before or heard in passing. Except for my personal journeys, which I will share pieces with you.

Real

Raw

And genuine.

What this book WILL do, is remind you, you are not alone and no matter where you are at or where you are starting from and with, there is a way out.

And that

My friend

IS ALWAYS THROUGH.

If you try to get around it any other way, it will keep coming to slap you silly and send you right back to the end of the line. I have witnessed it countless times in my career coaching thousands of clients. THE "I'll start over Monday" contagion would infect almost all of them at one point or another.

I could predict the days of the hardcore attempts to win the weekend battle of booze, junk food, sleeping in and slacking on the dreams they had begged to begin.

Monday was a hot mess showing up to every class, every session, tracking every morsel with the No Mercy Monday Mindset I had hounded in them. Tuesday was tough love with my truth-telling tactics that had people powerfully pushing through challenges - my ladies were putting on their big girl panties and my boys were engaging their most inner manly man beast modes. They MORE than showed up on Tuesday. They roared like lions and fought with a ferocious appetite to better their best from Monday. AND then...

Wednesday hit...

And...

They skipped.

Overslept.

Were too sore.

Too tired.

Too busy.

Needed a break.

I scoffed at their need for a break after just three days of thirty-minute workouts. Insert eye roll emoji here PLUS the red-faced angry guy emoji snaring both nostrils AND might as well throw in the curse word emoji too while we are at it OR I might drop another F-bomb.

I worked 17-hour days, six days a week, sometimes seven days never shutting it off to build a business (break-free) for the first 4 years.

"I can't even" was my typical response to the countless text messages that explained excuses my eyes were tired of rolling from. Wednesday was the ONE day of the week where I wanted them to Wake the Warrior within.

To Fight.

TO DO it Anyways.

To force themselves past the pain.

To rise.

To roar.

But mostly,

They slacked.

I was disappointed every time. And every time, I shouted passionately WTF!

In my head and out loud.

Believe it or not, saying I told you so, isn't something I ever wanted to say as a coach.

I wanted them to see it. To know it. To bleed for it. Like I had. But come Thursday, their participation in their own life was hit or miss. And Friday, was the last call to mythically pre-burn the calories they had been craving in their head as they counted down the hours to their booze-chugging-end-of-the-workweek-I-hate-my-job-my-life-sucks happy hour.

By Saturday there was a cluster of regulars, newbies and OH WOW! It's so good to finally see you, agains.

NOW

I will say, SOME did stay solid.

On point. Persistent. Focused. Determined. And Relentless.

They patiently waited for their turn at the front of the line. They were ready to be awarded their new life. They had made their machetes and came in hot swinging left and right. These guys were the 1%. My high-fiving favorites that fed on the right fuel. Their faith. Their fortitude. And their future self.

But mostly

One-by-one

I watched people with so much potential make their way from three-quarters of the way there, like you are so fucking close to the front of the line, don't you dare go back and start all over again.

But then they did.

Lose 20 lbs. Gain it all back.

Leave the relationship, then go back.

Stop smoking, then go back.

Get off the bottle, then go back.

Bounce around from thing to thing to thing, Except the RIGHT THING.

Then go back.

I got angry.

A lot.

One of my one-percenters once told me, You're not angry -You're just passionate.

So, I AM.

Smirk.

Smile.

Nod.

With gritted teeth, I watched them, one-by-one, as they began falling backwards in line forfeiting their turn to take hold of the very reason they started in the first place.

A better life.

Watching it was an unforgiving, frustrating, and painful process for me as a coach and as a human who had fought so hard to be standing within those four walls. To be standing period. I had fought a hard fight in another life that I'll soon tell you about. A fight that nearly killed me and forced me to start over in a line I never thought I would ever have to be in. So, watching them squander away their chance at a new beginning at better - was beyond infuriating for me. It was a slow motion breaking of my heart for theirs.

They could not UNLEARN their impatience. They could NOT stop their craving for a quick fix. Their grit to stay in the game was NOT the same type of grit my grandfather had instilled in me. It blew my mind that they didn't see or know or realize the chance they had. The opportunities they had. That the possibilities were there for them. Right there for the taking. But nobody was taking.

I lost sleep at night. Lying awake wondering why. Eventually, I concluded they hadn't been knocked down hard enough. They didn't know what hungry was. They didn't have a clear enough future ahead. They didn't know faith. They hadn't really felt the depths of loss. They had never had to grieve their old life. At least not YET.

So, they went back to the end of the line on Sunday night and would begin the cycle all over again on Monday morning. I never stopped praying for them to see their own faith in their potential. At least getting back in line, meant a piece of them still had some sense of HOPE that this next time could be the miracle of winning the messes in their minds and they would FINALLY stick with it and get to the front of the line.

What choices could you make today that would cease your start over cycle? What is one thing you could do today that would be a different choice than you normally choose? What would whacking down a new way mean for you? What freedom would it give you? What peace? What joy? What pursuit would you end up living in IF you ever got to the front of your line?

stuck

A Fixed State of Being

A Feeling of Overwhelming Incapacity

The Art of Watching Life Pass You By

The Knowing of Choosing Less Than

ROBYN MCLEOD THRASHER

your **BS**

they are the dirty little secrets
that keep egging you on and
telling you its ok to go back to
the back of the line

Now,   we have all started over.

And over.

And over.

And gotten back in line a fair share of times.

We've established it means you haven't given up. That you still have a fighting chance.

Yay. Awesome. Go you.

BUT eventually YOU WILL have to STOP stopping.

The line will just keep getting longer each time and your long list of BS will be the bodyguard blocking you from moving forward if you don't stay steady in your conviction to your commitments rather than your circumstances.

NOW, let's talk about this BS. It isn't what you think it is.

Well kind of.

Sort of.

Your BS are the Bad Stories you tell yourself. So ultimately it is your bullsh$!

It's your excuses.

It's your reasonings.

It's your logic from like decades ago that is ancient and outdated.

It's your I'll blame it on my childhood trauma story.

Your long-ago I used to be the high school star story.

The you-are-still-living-in-your-college-shenanigans story.

The I had kids too young so I couldn't finish school story.

The I got married to a jerk story.

The I'm a single mom-dad story.

The I don't know how story.

It's ALL the I'm too old, too fat, too tired, too broke, too broken, too washed-up stories.

The it's too hard story.

I don't have enough time story.

The doctor told me I can't story.

Your Bad Stories are freaking fairy tales that got stuck at the climax where the wicked witch and vengeful warrior capture your thoughts and feelings and actions and beliefs and holds you hostage from the happy never-ending story.

Your BS is YOUR stuck in your own nightmare story.

YOUR bad stories are the excuses you have trained your brain to believe above all else. You see problems rather than possibilities. You see pain rather than empowerment.

They are the dirty little secrets that keep egging you on and telling you its ok to go back to the back of the line. That starting over isn't THAT bad.

But that's just the I haven't given up yet story, BUT I'm not exactly doing my best YET either story.

Bad Stories are your go-to reasons for anything and everything in your life that scares the shit out of you or challenges you or pursues you or questions you or demands you to show up for something bigger than the you – YOU are right now.

Your BS tells you to stop one whack too soon - fearful that another swing might mean you might actually succeed and leave all the BS behind you.

Your Bad Stories are born from your previous upsetting experiences. Your cry me a river it didn't go my way stories. It wasn't my fault stories. I couldn't help it stories. It is what it is stories. Experiences that you had hoped would be romantic and dreamy and happily-ever-after stories, but instead left you abandoned, rejected, confused, lost and questioning your self-worth and whether or not you actually have something good enough to offer and give to this world, much less to yourself, stories.

Your BS doesn't do the job you think it does. In fact, they are thrifty thieves in the middle of day. Stealing your persistence and perseverance as the sun is shining brightly in your face. They snatch up your potential and passion and purpose in broad daylight, and you are powerless to stop it because you believe more in your BS than you do in opening your eyes to the beauty of the sun's rays, beaming down on you, lighting the path perfectly designed for imperfect you.

Getting past them is no easy feat, I get that. It's been piling up for years. And you've memorized all the pain.

Hell, you're mesmerized by it.

But IT IS possible to change their ending. To rewrite a new chapter that doesn't end in defeat. To tell a NEW capable YOU story.

That it CAN happen FOR you story.

The - I did it story.

All you gotta do is pick up your machete and start whacking and whacking and whacking and whacking until your bleeding from the inside out BECOMES your NEW fuck-off-all-you-negative-limiting-lying-stories-I got-this-new-beginning-story.

This one is a doozy. Scribble all your BS here. Let it all out. Leave nothing left inside. Write and write until you have squeezed all the BS out of your life. Do you see a pattern? A theme? What commonalities do they have? Do you think you're missing out on a better version of you because of the stories you've been telling yourself? Do you see the dirtiness in the four-letter words of L-I-E-S now? Do you see you're allowed to make a new choice? That you can tell a new story? And The choice I leave you with is not Can You? But Will You?

trapped

A Shutting of the Door on Your Life

An Allowing of Circumstances to Delay

Your Being

The Art of Accepting What Is

When It Is Truly Not

A Knowing of Immovable Indecision

whispering **screams**

**an alarm alerting you that there is more inside
you... more capability... more creativity... more
capacity... more doing... more living... more loving**

I believe every single one of us is living with a second life trapped inside and it is secretly screaming for you to help it escape its captivity from the chains of your fears and unbelief.

I think this scream is your inside life. THE LIFE muted by the BS we've been putting ourselves to sleep with. Walking around dead inside. Numb. Meh. Blah. Ambivalent. Indifferent. Exhausted from keeping up the appearance that the life you're living is the one you want.

You're not fooling anyone except yourself. You're *Walking Dead*-like except prettier with fake filters, false eye lashes and glowing up your social media sites like life is beautiful and bountiful. Except it isn't. Behind the lens you're dying a slow death inside. Losing passion. Losing hope. And most importantly, losing time. And no NOT everyone with fake eyelashes is living a false life. I'm just saying...

THE LIFE is the one you're really created to live for and through, BUT it's gotten muddied in the filth from your past as you've been forging through half ass beaten down paths living the life you've been USED TO, rather than the one you that was intended and built especially FOR you.

I THINK these screams are mistaken for whispers.

They are that soft quiet voice in our inner ear faintly fussing something about being able to do more than you currently are. An alarm alerting you that there is more inside you. More capability. More creativity. More capacity. More doing. More living. More loving.

I think these screams are so deep down in the depths of the filth inside our souls that when we actually hear it for the first time, they sound like faint whispers because they are buried so deep under layers and piles and secret passageways of past choices that feel very much like painful memories of things that can't come undone.

And you're stuck under the heaviness of it all.

But make no doubt, it's a fucking blood curdling scream. And it's your lifeline for your future. It's your legacy calling. It's your stories you have not YET lived. It is your authentic life trapped, trying to breathe and break free from a deathbed wish list THAT it doesn't want to be on.

Now I know that sounds morbid, but someone must hit you with the truth, or you'll wake up one day wondering what life you were supposed to live.

And wondering, is this it?

If you don't let the screams out, the answer will be yes. Absolutely. This life you're living now –

This

Is

It.

Rising into your resilience is all about paying attention to what you've already got within you, everything you've already come out of, and freed yourself from. It's your own fishhook machete whacking ways. You just have to dig up and out to let it be free.

The scream should sound like your favorite song, deafening you with all its dreaming possibilities and it CAN actually happen actualities. This song is anything Stevie Nicks for me just in case you needed a song to imagine in your mind for the movie-like life we are making.

This song should be heard from miles away with the windows rolled down and the wind blowing through your hair.

Yet we aren't turning up the volume to hear its between the line lyrics that would ultimately lure you out of your middle of the line place and fast track you to the fucking front.

So why aren't you blasting it?

Why are you muffling it?

Because it scares you?

Because it can't be guaranteed?

Because what will they think?

Because it will be hard?

Because you might break a sweat?

Because you might get sanctified in the process?

Because of what you will have to leave behind?

Because that kind of life is for other people?

Because THOSE dreams we've been hoarding in our hearts come true for her and for him, but definitely NOT for you or us?

What?

What?

Listen to yourself.

Seriously.

Listen.

Because you think cautiously about all the what ifs that could go wrong rather than all what ifs that WILL go right?

Living a life, we love. Embracing and overcoming our adversities. Unlocking our dreams.

That should NOT sound crazy. Yet it does. So, we shut it down before we even begin. And when I say "we," I mean YOU.

Quit effing running in the opposite direction of your dreams. Quit turning down the volume on your life. Quit explaining your lackluster excuses. Stop silencing the scream in charge of introducing you to your TRUE self.

We sabotage the survival of our own screams, shushing them back down into the darkness and in a rush, we hurry ourselves back to the end of the line to start over again.

Come on.

Not.

This.

Time.

Choose Different.

Fight for it.

Find your Freedom.

Your Peace.

Your Joy.

Your Fulfillment.

Your Happiness.

Your Gratitude.

No more complaining.

No more suffering.

No more whining.

No more settling.

I can't tell you how many times I have sabotaged my own success. My own strength. My own solitude. My own serenity and serendipitous moments because I'd been too busy trying to fight for the old life. Thankfully, my Machete Mentality that moved in at childhood has remained a steadfast roommate, giving me a scrappy resourceful incessant and relentless NEED to find a way even with all the self-induced sabotaging.

And I share that with you BODLY in this book. All the steps you need to release the life screaming at you inside. To live in your favorite song. To dance every morning with hope and possibility. And believe it or not, YOU are well on your way if you are doing the choose your own adventures questions at the end of each chapter. I know it's not quite the same. I can't rewrite two different endings for you or even tell you which path to whack down first. BUT You Can.

You can change course.

You can choose different.

You can be prepared.

Equipped with your Faith rather than your BS and armed with your mental machete rather than your excessive excuses.

Life is coming for you. Barreling down. Pretty effing fast too. And I want you to win. I want you to be roaring for it. Filthy and all. Showing up ugly and hungry. God doesn't need you to wash yourself clean before walking through the threshold of His home. Besides, we got your Ivory soap waiting for you after you're ready to start believing in your screams and turning the dial up, maxing out your listening capacity.

What is the scream inside of you saying? What is stopping you from answering it? Have you even truly tried to dig it up and out? How long are you going to let it play on repeat in your head? Like that catchy showtune or commercial jingle that gets stuck in our head, it's not going to let up until you start singing a new song. So, what makes you so different that all things are NOT possible FOR YOU? Do you think God overlooked you? He surely did not and has something amazing waiting for you to receive too. What is it about yourself that does not feel worthy, willing and capable of handling, managing and living the life trapped inside? You keep choosing to muffle it. Do you like the irritation of knowing it will never go away until you turn volume up and start singing out loud?

A Feeling of Sinking Slowly

A Living Without Hope

The Art of Making Temporary Permanent

A Knowing of Giving Up

ROBYN MCLEOD THRASHER

stuck settling

**there is a boiling in your blood to be more
when you come face-to-face with the
impermanence of your own existence**

Stuck and Settling.

Meet the fraternal twins typically joined at the hip. These two yahoos are often misunderstood and mistaken as interchangeable identical pairs. However, make no mistake, they are worlds apart.

Stuck says I don't know which way to go. I got this far, but I'm overwhelmed by the choices ahead, so I'm gonna stay here awhile.

Settling says I gave up. I've waved my white flag and have conceded my run in this race.
It's too much impossibility for me at this pace.

Stuck says Help! While Settling shouts GO AWAY. Leave me alone.

Stuck says MAYBE and at least contemplates calculating one more move. While Settling says NOPE, sits down and crosses its defiant arms with a scowl on its face.

Stuck shyly says I wanna give it another go, hesitating, YET secretly waiting to get put back in the game.

While Settling has boldly pronounced its objectives to any alternatives and waves away any other possibility of powering through the problem in its way.

Stuck STILL wants a chance to see. While Settling sees roadblocks and lives hopelessly in place.

So, are you Stuck?

Or

Are you Settling?

I can guarantee, you're one or the other somewhere in your life. You might even be caught up in between both. They can gang up on you. Bulling you into a beatdown to become best friends with each.

SO, ARE YOU?

Stuck somewhere?

Caught on your couch, *Netflix* binging with a bowl of chips crowding your mind with countless hours of other people's dreams, problems, dramas, issues NUMBING out from the reality that it's either all too much ALL at once - OR not enough Enough of the time?

I would be doing this with peanut butter M&M's and a glass of red wine. Just in case you needed another visual to stimulate your senses for the Hallmark movie I'm claiming we make one day.

But seriously?

Are you weighed down with hopelessness OR just I don't know how to start this?

Are you still wishing for more?

Or have you succumbed to the sacrificing of living any other way?

That this is it.

Life as is.

A used up, beat up, run down, foreclosed on home that isn't worth investing in anymore?

Eight years ago, I almost lost my life.

When I say almost, I mean, I should have died.

That experience gives you an urgency to life.

A, you-are-not-promised- tomorrow-maybe-not-even-all-of-today, URGENCY to life.

There is a boiling in your blood to BE MORE when you come face-to-face with the impermanence of your own existence.

Since that day, when God said to me, Nope - NOT just yet... My reverence for living illuminated my eyes to the environment I was coming up second place in. The life I was settling in. The life I was suffering in. Secretly.

At the exact same time, I almost lost my life, my second mom did lose hers.

God pulled me aside from the line to heaven above and He took her instead.

I got to go get back in line with a new mission and a new sense of just how limited, valuable, precise and powerful the life trapped inside of us is.

BUT she didn't.

I was awakened to both the blessing and the burden brought upon by her going and my being left behind. It's a daily struggle between guilt and purpose. Both fighting for the living. And more desperately for Him.

So yeah.

Nothing pisses me off more than settling. Not even traffic outside my five-mile radius or slow walking people.

Just settling people.

Waiting people.

Delaying people.

Choosing stuck and choosing settling people.

It's an angry button push for me.

It's a pain that surfaces immediately in me when I see people settling.

Because I KNOW, the ghost of her would grab your shoulders and shake the sense of revering LIFE into you.

It ignites an unfathomable, incomprehensible knowledge that only that level of grief and grace can bring to the table. That whatever life you are living – IT is merely leased.

When she died and I didn't, I started seeing life differently.

My home life.

My personal life.

My family life.

My childhood life.

My face in the mirror life.

My everything that had once been life.

I was ashamed and I hated what I saw.

So many choices wrong.

So many mistakes unseen.

So many hidden giants buried inside my screams.

After her death, I couldn't help but to look at the people encircling me and see the level of sadness as they stuck in their settling too.

It was everywhere.

Like I had new eyesight for seeing the blind for the very first time.

I saw a double fucking whammy of both in the same place.

Side-by-side, neck-and-neck, there they lived in between two worlds that were sinking them slowly. Stuck in a world much like the upside-down one in *Stranger Things*, except this upside-down world is a sad reality MOST never get out alive from.

No fucking way was I going out like that.

He didn't save me for nothing. She didn't die for me to squander the happiness she wanted me to go find.

When I was granted the gift of getting off my deathbed, the whispers inside me screamed out in full glory.

A Warriors Cry.

An Altar Call.

A Hail Mary, please save me. Don't leave me here begging for a new beginning. Take me with you. Don't leave me behind.

So wide awake and running from the comfort of them both, I had to scan through my own BS for Stuck and Settling coming for me with no remorse. They liked the comfort of crying inside. But my second chance started showing up like it was a Tough Love Tuesday and it was next up to take its rightful place in the front of the line.

I could see my life flashing before my eyes. The people I loved. The people I helped. The people I hurt. The way I was raised. The way I was loved. The way I was unloved. The way I was taught. The way I was left to fend for myself. The way they handled hard. The way I didn't. The way I was expected to show up a certain way. The way I was expecting someone else to show up for me.

I could see all the pain and hurt and anger and shame and sadness and suffering swirling around me and them.

So, I armored up for my new life. Rehearsing again and again my rebuke of the things I had seen and been and known.

Because she isn't here, I would fight different.

Because they are, I would live different.

Because he stands on the street and sells water for $1, I would forgive him.

Because his rage stood before me and I saw evil in his eyes, I would pray for him.

Because he left me in a job, I would make one myself that never did the same.

Because she always did her best, I would strive to do better.

Because he could fix everything with grey tape and zip ties, I would repeat the same.

Because he lost his temple to temptation, I would nourish mine with good nutrition.

Because she choose to talk herself into an early death, I would speak vitality over mine.

Because he is dead sitting in that chair, I would walk around alive in adventuring.

Because he lost himself encouraging and enabling her, I would rid myself of co-dependency.

Because he never saw me for more than just an exotic escape, I would replace lust with love.

Because she lost years being shy to her shame, I would face my giants and live authentically.

Because I know life is undoubtedly on borrowed time, I would always choose to BE HERE NOW.

In this moment.

In a knowing that yesterday is gone and tomorrow will never come for me. I choose Better not because theirs wasn't good enough, but because settling must settle somewhere. And that was not going to be with me or mine.

I died somewhere in my multiple hospital stays. I don't know where exactly. ICU. Operating table. Hallway waiting for testing. Corridor in a wheelchair sitting in agony as I awaited painful PT to learn to walk again. Hospital bed with three tubes draining sickness out of me. Somewhere in between all the ambulance rides. I don't know when it happened, but I know I never came back from that. And I thank God daily because I was on a fast track to dark desperate places where lies thrived and your dignity died.

Now, I don't want YOU to have to have a near-death experience to stop settling or lose a loved one to wake you the fuck up. That's a slice of your soul that never gets replaced. You don't have to stay settled in what was or what is, accepting last minute leftovers and scraping by with second best.

But I'll be honest though... Sometimes, I don't even know how the hell I got here.

But I do know, one day I woke up and walked past the stranger in the mirror and was finally able to say good morning to myself for the first time in way too many years.

She smiled back and we've been a team ever since.

But it was years of seeing that stranger stare back at me. Washing her face. Applying her mascara. Brushing her teeth. Glimpsing up awkwardly and shyly and shamefully just to see if she would respond with a nod of knowing someday, SOMEDAY surely, she would be ok.

But it never came. Not until recently.

The hardest part of living after your almost death, is accepting you would never be the same anyways. And you would never get a chance to say goodbye to the life you were forced to leave behind.

BUT right now...

You still have a choice.

You have time and opportunity to make new choices that bring better decisions.

That can awaken you. That can rise up in you. That can bloom something new inside of you.

You have a chance, to say goodbye. To grieve that last life. To say see you later with a wave and a wink knowing you never will.

You have a choice.

And I am begging YOU to choose the You inside of You.

When was the last time you could face the stranger making eyes at you in the mirror? Wondering who the hell you are? Where did you go? When will you ever come back? Are you at peace with this person? Or at war? And what is encircling your space? What's the energy? What's the drive? Is it more stuck? Is it more settling? Or maybe you've got more fight figuring its way out? What resonates about this life for you? And what needs to be rid from it? What needs to be derived from it?

lies

A Sneaky Story that Deceives

An Irreversible Truth that Steals Your Dignity

The Art of Losing Yourself

A Knowing that Binds You to

Senseless Battlefields

ROBYN MCLEOD THRASHER

skinny **mirror**

they will tell you anything you want to believe...
and show you anything you want to see

Walmart sells a skinny mirror for $10. It's AMAZING for your ego. It's long and tall and gives the illusion you're about three inches taller and 10 lbs. thinner than you truly are.

Then there is the dressing room department store mirror that slaps you awake with their big ass square block mirrors in dull yellow low lighting that make you look 10 lbs. wider, three inches shorter and ten years older.

I thought mirrors weren't supposed to lie to you. BUT they do. They will tell you anything you want to believe. And show you anything you want to see.

Hear me out.

The Walmart mirror - YOU KNOW - this is a lie.

You know you aren't suddenly three inches taller and skinner. BUT you purposely take the selfie in that mirror to appear to be this way. You see what you want. You stare at this version of you – this version you want – but aren't quite willing to keep showing up for because its hard. Hard to get there and hard to keep it up there.

NOW, the department store mirror is just as bad. It's showing you the worst version of you – the version you choose to see regardless of the crappy lighting and fat squared mirrors. NOW, you know no one looks good in that light YET you walk out feeling depressed and sad and fat and old, knowing that truth isn't the truth either.

It's all about what you CHOOSE to see.

We see what we want when we look at our lives. We can see good. Or we can see all our bad. We can see effort, or we can see excuses. We can see better. Growth. Different. Or we can see falling short, stuck in a rut, and the same old, same old you.

I studied journalism in junior high, high school and college for many years. I was recruited young and rose quickly through the ranks as yearbook editor-in-chief, co-editor and managing editor. I did it all. Loved it all. Thrived in it all. Except for the grammar part of it all. Ha. Ha. Ha.

It's still very much a part of me. And it was where I learned the five W's & H theory, I play out in almost every area of my life today.

In journalism, to get the story, the whole story, not just some snapshot Cliff notes version, we were taught to ask the:

Who

What

When

Where

Why

and HOW did I fucking get here in everything we did?

Ok, sooooo we didn't ask that last little part, but I'm asking you to NOW.

These questions ensured we weren't JUST getting the skinny mirror story or the fat mirror story. These simple questions guaranteed FACTS. Truth. Unbiased pieces of a puzzle that you could put together to write a captivating, inspiring or educating story. A story that would explain and give characters a place to go and dream. A story that would share all the details, not just display the parts we wanted to see or hear.

These simple questions can breakdown the barriers holding you back. They can reveal an unseen dream. They can alert you to an Oprah moment that flips your switch and helps you see a fresh perspective. They can untangle the WHY you ARE stuck. And they can DIG out the HOW to make your way out.

So, let's practice:

Who?

Who were you? Who are you? Who do you want to become? Who do you love? Who do you show up for? Who do you serve? These questions can powerfully transform you one way or the other. The old you. The today you. OR the YOU - waiting on you.

Yes, this space is for you to actually do the work:

What?

What happened? What will you do it about? What will happen next? What decision will make you or break you or take you down a different path? What way can you improve yourself? What skill can you learn and build and adopt into your daily habits? What habits got you here? What behaviors will get you there? What do you want? What do you need? What do you deserve? What are you worth?

This space too:

When?

When are you going to step up? When are you going to let go? When are you going to take action? When are you going to forgive yourself? When will you see the good in you versus the bad? When will you progress? When will you give grace? When will you let faith take over and let fear subside? When will you start showing up for your future self? When will you give it all over to God's amazing grace?

I'll leave extra space here....

Where?

Where did it all go wrong? Where did it all go right? Where do you want to go from here? Where do you see yourself when you look in the mirror? Where will you be if you keep acting like a jerk to yourself? Where will you be if you shape up and start fighting for yourself? Where is this life taking you? Where do you want to be taken to? Where do you want to be delivered from?

Little more space here... keep answering...you have time...

Those seem easy enough.

Don't they?

Did you interact there?

Make SURE you answer those bad boys or we can't move forward creating new stories for YOUR NEW self.

And we are NOT STAYING STUCK.

. . .

NOW, for Why and How, I'm going to give you a little help. This is where we usually get caught up. Stuck in the WHY did this happen? Why didn't it happen? HOW did I effing get here? HOW can I ever get out?

We bounce back and forth between them both like a bad game of ping pong that never ends. Aching our heads and hearts with problematic questions that sometimes cannot even EVER be answered and it's in the Acceptance of this WHERE you will find your NEW story.

So How?

How did you end up here?

Stuck.

Settling.

Suffering.

Lying.

Dying inside?

Well, your standards suck.

Your boundaries are borderless.

And you live in complete chaos.

You have no structure. You have no oomph. No grit. No gumption.

You're caught up in contemplating all the reasons WHY, rather than focusing your attention on all the WAYS you can still move forward in spite of and anyways.

You aren't looking for a way through. You're looking for way to excuse yourself from showing up for life. And using the HOW did this ever happen like a whoa-is-me-damsel-in-distress is so old school I CAN'T EVEN...

Wake. The. Eff. Up.

It doesn't matter HOW. Not for this story. At least not right now.

The ONLY How you need to know, is HOW will you handle your Sh$! From here on out? How will you MOVE forward? How will you start NOW, today, showing up for your future self?

And Why?

I think, you got knocked down and got back up, but you didn't wipe off the filth and are secretly saving the hurt and anger and resentment from it all as a souvenir of some sort.

Then I think you got knocked down again, got back up like you did before, but this time a little more pissed off. A little more winded. A little more WTF? A little more I just got up. A little more WHY me? Why now? Why again?

You tuck away these resentful remnants in your back pocket. And you hang on to their bitterness and then start to bite back.

You didn't acknowledge what happened. You didn't even accept it. And certainly, didn't adapt to it whatever it was. And YOU think you should get some after school extra credit participation award because you at least stood back up. BUT you don't deserve shit. None of us do. So, you get bitter and resentful and tack on a new BS to your laundry list of lies. Then the cycle repeats itself AND repeats itself

And repeats itself

And repeats itself.

Why?

Well,

because YOU let it.

Eventually, it wears you down and your endurance exits the story you've been walking through. You sigh and then you stay right there in the midst of HOW and WHY in a fucking ping pong game you don't belong in.

You stay put like snoozing in bed on a cold morning, snuggling up in the sheets just a little while longer WHEN you know you need to get up. YOU KNOW where you are at IS not serving you. You know your time under the covers has expired. You know you're not winning this game.

Make no mistake.

You ARE well aware.

You ARE.

But you stay anyway, and you ignore the screaming inside that is urging you to move because it's comfy.

It's safe.

It's certain.

And it doesn't hurt as bad as getting knocked back down again. So, you justify your laziness and staying stuckness until one day you catch the stranger running from its reflection and you realize it stopped smiling a long time ago.

And if you're offended by laziness.

Good.

You probably are being lazy somewhere in your life otherwise you wouldn't be Stuck, Settled or Suffering. Because getting out of those states requires effort and effort doesn't do business with laziness.

SO, get the fuck up.

You've lost yourself.

You've checked out and checked into a treadmill routine of just getting by and surviving the day, counting down the hours to clock out. Wishing away the week and wasting away every weekend, drowning in whatever it is that fills you up SO you can escape the emptiness inside, hoping to drown out the screams barely getting past your whiney stuck and settling outside cries.

YOU have given up

Yes, you have.

I hear you.

I hear you saying, But.

BUT, my back is up against the wall.

My Bills

My Rent

My Mortgage

My Kids

My Obligations

My Responsibilities

My Job

My Time

Yeah

Yeah

Yeah

I hear you

I also hear violins

Don't be a baby

Listen up.

Staying Stuck will have you WISHING for more BUT not ever fully acting on it. It will have you living with regrets and wanting more but never going for it.

And Settling limits your beliefs. Closes your mind and perspectives to the BS you tell you yourself every damn day. Settling says I'm right and Your dreams are wrong. It is walking around with a sad grin that is secretly saying just go away because IT IS going through the motions unnecessarily numb.

It is not living in your full potential. Well, who the hell knows what your full potential is anyways? I don't know.

But God.

Maybe He is the scream inside us all. He's got to be the only one that knows for sure what we are all totally capable of. But I still believe that we know - that you know - whether or not YOU are truly pushing through to your potential OR just settling in the fact that you might have some.

Do you REALLY just want to have potential? Or do you ACTUALLY want to experience the freedom in exposing it?

Settling IS protecting that potential because exposing it is risky. Exposing it would mean making new choices, new changes and new commitments.

Exposure would take effort AND effort needs endurance AND endurance rises only from your own resilience AND resilience doesn't roommate with someone shrinking in their own sad story of settlement.

So, you choose your own adventure here. I think we've already asked enough questions.

purpose

A Reason to Keep Going In Spite of All the

Reasons to Not

An Unstoppable Pursuit for Serving Him

The Art of Living Outside of Yourself

A Knowing in Honor Your Value

relentless resilience

**if you want something badly enough, you
will craft the necessary tools you need in the
contents of your character to make it happen**

Now you must be wondering, how does she expect me to RISE into Superwoman like resiliency when I'm stuck in my own messed up mess?

And WHAT does that even mean?

Rise into Resiliency?

Great question. See. You are learning to ASK.

Look,

You've been settling because you don't have resilience in your confidence arsenal. You can't fight back because you don't know how OR you've long forgotten the amount of brilliantness already built inside of you in the midst of all your messes.

You can't see it right now. You are too close. You are too tired. You are too discouraged. You are too busy. You are too overwhelmed. You are too beat up from your BS.

But I see past all that. That stuff is minutia to me. AND remember...I told you... I'm the girl that rolls up her sleeves, finds a way to make a way and will wave you forward with me.

I got you. So, let's go.

"A dream forces you to develop the skills you don't have."

I love this quote. It's anonymous and unknown to me, but this author is spot on here.

So, let's let that sink in.

"A dream forces you to develop the skills you don't have."

If you want something badly enough, YOU will craft the necessary tools you need in the contents of your character to make it happen.

That's The Machete Mentality.

Think it.

See it.

Believe it.

Speak it.

Find a way for it.

Make a way through TO it.

Practice it.

Exercise it.

Refine it.

And then do it again, but BETTER.

You can create it from the filth you've already fought.

You can build it from the BS you've exposed and evicted from your heart talk.

You can borrow it from your bruises that beat you down previously.

You can fuel it with new energy, new effort and the eager excitement having the right encouragement brings.

I promise you this book is not a websters dictionary knockoff with all these definitions, BUT just bear with me as we dig a little deeper.

Resiliency keeps you from giving up on yourself And IF you don't give up on yourself, YOU won't be what? That's right.

Settling.

Suffering.

Stuck.

Resiliency is your weapon when life tries to stop you dead in your tracks.

Resiliency is how you take the punches.

It's How YOU Respond.

It's How YOU React.

It's YOU Showing up Ugly. Perfectly imperfect. In spite of. Regardless. Anyway.

It's YOU laying down all the excuses and giving your washed-up explanations a good *Steel Magnolia's* Weezer slap.

Resilience is finding reasons to go on rather than regurgitating reasons why you can't. It is keeping the consistency in spite of setbacks. It is enduring patiently. It is pushing yourself but pacing yourself. It is always being in the driver's seat AND buckling your feelings tightly in the back.

Resiliency is forging forward in your filth. It's standing on your mountain finally determined to clear your path for all that potential you've placed on pause.

Resiliency is how you keep going WHEN the face of adversity is as giant as Goliath, standing before you, standing in the midst of you, AND standing in the aftermath of you.

Realizing you and Goliath... Y'all are one in the same... And oh what a web we can weave.

Let me tell you a story about me making my mess intentionally and then rising up from its humble ashes in an aftermath only God could predict.

I knew the day was coming. I just didn't know exactly when. But I KNEW it was coming for me like a strong wind necessary to whip me into place.

I had been on the phone for months trying to resolve a way to stay longer in our overpriced rental home that I could never really afford in the first place, but I wanted the house with the pool for the kids more than my ego could muster up the righteousness to say no.

I was in the middle of a separation and a divorce and had just uprooted my safety and sanity to move jobless with my two young kids to Florida where their father, my then soon-to-be ex-husband, had moved for a job.

I knew upon signing the leasing documents, I would never be able to afford it. I had nothing. No money except for what wasn't even awarded to me yet in the divorce decree.

And I didn't have a job because I had a dream.

Build a business. Own a gym.

I got this, I said.

Somehow, I pulled it off for nearly a year and a half barely making the rental house payments. Living on credit cards and using up every bit of my 50% of his 401k. My second dad said don't do it. You don't have a clue. And he was 100000% fucking right.

I didn't have a clue.

But who am I?

Yep.

I'm the girl that is going to do it anyways.

I'll machete that shit.

Make it fucking happen.

And somehow, I did.

My ex-partner and I built the business from the ground up. From our imaginations to a tiny ass garage, to a dirt field, to a turnkey brick and mortar fancy retail spot perfectly waiting for us in the heart of my hometown.

Month-after-month, scraping by with pennies. Legit, somedays piggy bank pennies paid the groceries as we cooked cheesy eggs day-after-day.

We gave every ounce of blood, sweat and tears for it and to it. We left nothing in our tank.

I gave every last dime to drive the dream from inside of our heads to a full-blown walk in the front door with music popping and people packed into every 2,000 square feet of that real life-fuck-yeah-holy-shit-we-did-it dream.

Curse words were totally necessary there. It was our movie moment. A dream, we literally had made up, was playing out before our very own unbelieving eyes.

Except we didn't work fast enough or smart enough or good enough.

While our endurance was indestructible emerging from early mornings, long days and what seemed like endless nights, we were always missing a piece. And no amount of our unstoppable Grit and Grind and Hustle could substitute for that missing magic that would have made our dream an empire and our empire our everything.

Client after Client

Hour after Hour

and back-to-back-to-back bills, brought back-to-back bickering and belittling and beatdowns on each other and on ourselves.

We were tormented in a tug of war of who should do what, when and where. We were fighting apart and fighting at each other instead of fighting for the dream that had once unified us like a *Marvel* dream team.

Every day I prayed for better. I prayed for hope. I prayed for a hand to hold that would walk with me and not against me.

All along I was too close to the situation, naively calling upon another human who had been hurt just as much as I had from a tender past. We were incapable of filling the missing piece no matter what we tried. And we had tried everything.

Business cards everywhere. Awkwardly walking parking lots placing flyers under windshield wipers only to see them one week later washed up and worn out in a gutter down the street. We invested in coaches and business classes, books, podcasts, seminars, networking and even set up decked out tables at pop-up markets and community events. It was no Kevin Costner's, build it and they will come *Field of Dreams*.

So, when the eviction notice was posted on our front door after we arrived home from teaching classes one night, we were shocked but not surprised. It's like knowing better, but not doing enough of better to make the knowing actually effective to bring about a change.

The notice was just like in the movies. Taped to our front door with a big fat sheriff's department stamp on it. I didn't even care what the neighbors thought. All I cared about was handling the next best step.

Find a way to make a way.

And YES, I had been paying the bills at the gym. A hefty $6,000 a month just to open the front door. Then I had been choosing our choices of what check would go where next.

Electric

Water

Food

Gas

Internet

Insurance

Advertising

Marketing

Software

There were more bills than money. And that was just the gym bills. They totaled sometimes $8,000, $10,000 and at one point $12k a month. I know it might not sound like a lot. BUT we had nothing.

Nuuuuuuuthing.

We had like negative nothing.

We started with just a dream and some dirt. But what it was – WAS enough soil to grow the forced skills we needed to create something out of nothing.

"A dream forces you to develop the skills you don't have."

We practiced selling. And marketing. And selling some more. We dreamed up new ways. We made new paths of programs and services to help, truly HELP, our clientele. And that rewarded us with some income to pay some bills.

So, we created more of what we could and paid the papers. Then we created again and paid the next set of papers. Then we created again and had a little ice cream. I mean it was a defeating cycle that deserved a little Cold Stone here and there. For a moment, we could relax and savor we were safe for another day, another week, sometimes another month.

BUT THEN... The home bills were another Giant we would fail to slay.

There weren't enough people. There wasn't enough revenue. There wasn't enough left of either of us to salvage our dream it seemed.

We had to choose daily.

BUT I never stopped knowing that our choosing of the dream was ever the wrong choice. So, we sacrificed our home and our ego and our ability to escape out into the excuses. We burned the *Tony Robbins* boat and set ourselves out alone on the island of hope.

The humbling, embarrassing eviction scarlet letter said we had 24 hours to pack, move and get the eff out. In my mind, a burly sheriff's deputy would be back shortly to escort us away and NO way in my little firecracker fierce mind was that ever going to fucking happen.

I don't think we ever worked so well together than in those 24 hours. Knowing that we would be homeless. Knowing we would be sleeping on the gym floor and NOT knowing for how long. Not even understanding what eviction meant in the long run or how we would ever get past it.

It's amazing what you can do when you band together in trauma, in tragedy, in turmoil and in tension. It's amazing what tenacity teamwork can build when you make a conscious decision to join forces.

And it was our mess. We constructed it consciously. Hoping we would outrun it. But, as you can see, we didn't.

One day later, we left behind half of my children's six-and-eight-year-old toys. We left behind a fancy French door refrigerator that I just had to have when I lived the life I was shrinking from and shaming myself into all kinds of lies.

I thought I had arrived when we bought that refrigerator. It was a symbol for me of a happy wife, happy life, happy home, but stocking it only filled me with a fleeting fix of happiness that always somehow felt more like emptiness.

We left behind furniture and clothes and so many things I can't even recall why they had been bought in the first place. It was a pathetic showing of these things that turned my stomach sick at the sight of them. I had once chosen to spend my hard-earned time on this stupid stuff that symbolized disposable dreams. SMH now. Crying then.

Yet, we still stuffed what we could into the smallest $200 a month storage unit. Another bill we didn't even know how or when it would even get paid. We packed our cars with our most favorite possessions. The valuables. The sentimentals. The breakables. The I can't do without-ables.

My kids not knowing the severity of the situation THEN, but fully knowing and understanding NOW the gravity of the grace that comes with losing it all, had asked when we were coming back.

Never I said.

And then we drove away.

We made that mess.

We chose it.

For a greater good.

For a breaking of generational curses that said we never could.

And we paid a price

That taught us

Resilience

Forgiveness

Grace

And a coming togetherness that you CANNOT ever replace.

I choke up writing this. Tears welling in my eyes as you read these words. A remembrance in my soul that cannot breathe. It is a healing that will never be and simply a part of me that just lives inside of me now.

For 6 months, we slept on the floor.

We slept on yoga mats and piled up towels for pillows and blankets. We slept on 6-inch flaky air mattresses that deflated the minute you laid your head down to forget the day and hope to God you got some rest.

My kids, thank the Lord, split their time between me and their dad, but during their time with me and without a single fuss, they shared a small twin mattress, sleeping head to foot in their prison-cell sized room.

I had whole-heartedly decorated one side unique for him and one side especially for her. Their pictures and paintings hung on each wall with their stuffed animals tucked neatly along the edges of the bed they shared. It wasn't much. But it was the nicest makeshift setup made with my unconditional love for them and for the future I was damned determined to build back better.

During the day, their room doubled as a playroom for clients' kids. That killed something inside of me. I cringed every time one of "them" trashed the room. Disrespecting the space, I had set up so nicely for my babies. I had painted the walls, hung curtains in a desperate attempt to provide privacy from the sliding glass doors that were more like a fishbowl tank exposing their personal space.

It was my ill attempt to disguise and protect MY kids' dignity every damn day. And "these other kids" bee-bopped around in it all carefree and disregarding. It made me nauseous with resentment, jealously and hatred not for them, but for me. It was the only safe space I had left in my own will and watching others walk all over it without ever knowing what that tiny little room represented for me was a torturous welling on my heart that weighed heavily on my motherly ego.

It was a long way from their two story, five-bedroom home in Georgia. There was no swimming pool or fancy playroom with Disney characters dancing on the walls. They didn't have their playhouse and sandbox or separate bedrooms. They had plastic storage containers for a dresser to hold a fraction of their clothes in. But I took pride in making this temporary space feel safe and secure. It was their sanctuary, protected with a mother's war cry and a perfectly imperfect dream that one day we would be restored through Him.

And YES. It could have been a lot worse. But this is MINE, not yours or theirs.

We thankfully had the gym and a roof over our head. We didn't sleep in the car or in the streets. We never had to go to the food pantry. But boy those piggy banks got wiped clean.

As a mother, I had hit rock bottom. What kind of mother chooses a dream over a job that could have easily paid the bills for a rental home with a swimming pool? How selfish was I? What kind of mother chooses faith over fear and steps into the unknown with two little responsibilities that hold your hand tightly no matter where you go?

I did.

And I kept on.

Naively?

Stupidly?

Probably so.

But I believed.

We cooked eggs on an electric skillet on top of a 6-foot folding table in the back office, which also converted hour-by-hour into a makeshift kitchen, a living room, a bathroom and a bedroom, plus a work office to do sales calls depending on the time of day it was.

At night, we hid from the landlord. Scared to death he would kick us out of the business space for sleeping there. We tip toed around hoping no one in the walls could hear us or see our most vulnerable and naked prayers on our knees.

We took birdbaths in a yucky double sink for several weeks. Using washcloths and baby wipes to dab us off. Joining the local LA Fitness to take a real shower or driving 30 minutes to my fathers for a getaway weekend to sleep in a real bed became a tropical vacation with hot water and bath towels that were fluffy and fuzzy and felt like heaven against our beat-up, worn-down bodies broken from the hours and hours of punishment our excessive personal training demanded from us.

We walked across the street to Walgreens for late night ice-cream treats and ordered takeout from Glory Days, but to this day my kids still love the New York Style pizza we ate most nights of the week from the mom-and-pop shop 100 feet away.

They celebrated their birthdays in that place. With balloons and a cake and presents that tried to make up for the lack of privacy, peace, and freedom that only your own home can house for you.

That day, for a few hours, we pretended everything was ok. Their cousins and grandparents came to celebrate them. While we were sitting around a folding table decorated with dollar store balloons and colorful plastic tablecloths, singing Happy Birthday and smiling, I was silently ashamed, and a sickening sadness wore inside me like your favorite pair of beat-up shoes.

As everyone else stood there laughing and chatting, I flashed back to their last birthday. A victorious pool party with friends from school. There was a gigantic water slide and party games, goodie bag treats and a bedroom of their own to show off. But here now, I was choking up on the weight of the wonder in that exact moment - that forced me into second-guessing every choice I had made had brought us HERE. In all my choices, THIS is what I had to show for all my sacrifice. A makeshift birthday party in a space where people, where strangers, had come to both lose and find themselves simultaneously. THIS is where I would have to honor my kids' births?

It was humiliating, humbling and it hurt like fucking hell. Worse than the hospital. Worse than the chronic pain. Worse than the tubes being pulled out of me. Worse than the medicine. Worse than the divorce. Worse than the eviction.

Worse than the lies that looked back at me in the mirror. This was rock bottoms - ROCK bottom.

They turned seven and nine in that place. Not knowing, but KNOWING, this wasn't how life was supposed to be. I want to tell you NOW how awesome and amazing my kids truly are because of THIS.

But that's another book another time another day with another outpouring of everything my heart can say. You can read all about it in Dancing with Tsunamis (my upcoming tell all, the why behind my machete ways, the story behind the story, the juicy in-depth details that rip open and dissect these mini snippet stories that are merely just pieces of me.)

Just KNOW, your kids build their resilience upon yours. They build their perspectives upon yours. They build their heart song and truths and beliefs of where they can go and who they can be or where they can't and what they won't ever even attempt to do - based upon yours. So, you better be building yours straight up rock steady. Choose your choices with them in mind. NOT solely for them, but certainly for their ability to see how well you can rise, so one day, they rise above and beyond you.

Now, in that place, we pretended for months. We acted. We hid. We ran a sham letting everyone believe we had more behind those red brick walls than we did. They had no idea that THIS was it for us. In fact, it even took several years long after we were out of it before we got comfortable and transparent telling the truth about our living arrangements that had us living IN our dream rather than for it.

That we had failed miserably at managing, planning, generating, budgeting, increasing, scaling, listening, doing and executing on the dream and instead had been dilly-dallying around with it hoping one day it would suddenly become a success story.

BUT we HAD succeeded in jumping.

In going for our dream.

In doing what others thought was crazy.

We thought was normal.

We HAD succeeded in enduring.

And showing up and rising up.

While we had failed in finding that missing piece to put us together, but we HAD discovered a freedom in knowing we could make something out of nothing and develop the skills along the way.

Owning a business was hard.

Running a business was harder.

Taking the hits of being run by your business was a torturous disaster.

Doing a dream takes a depth of determination that feeds off failure after failure after failure.

And the ability to face them, fix them and to keep going is a test that will only succeed if you are listening to the right screams.

At the time, we were both pushing it down back inside. We didn't know. We didn't see it then and we certainly couldn't hear it over the noises of stress and struggle and setbacks surrounding our minds and misgivings.

It would have been so easy to quit.

To give up.

To make excuses and to blame.

But we kept going.

We rose up.

We became Relentless.

We became Resilient for finding a way.

To MAKING a way.

Through it all.

I have long forgotten a lot of what it felt like to live there. I truly don't remember how bad it was because I think we made the best of it. Or I've blocked the bullshit and pull only from the power of it. I didn't lose everything on purpose to lose everything on purpose. That serves a fight in me NOW that gets me up faster every damn time I screw up to this day.

I see the sacrifice of it all now and the hurt and the pain and the constant desire to endure another day as a rite of passage most entrepreneurs experience. It's almost part of the package when you sign up to birth a dream and begin living in it and with it.

It's an expected pain you must be willing to take.

Not long after we made our gym our home, my fancy way-overpriced-could also-never-really-afford-it-but-look-at me-driving-it SUV was repossessed from our substitute driveway. The same parking lot that had served as a foundation for gritty, you can take it, toughen up, don't be a baby, suck it up buttercup, tire-flipping, walking lunges, suicide sprints and team building beatdowns SUDDENLY became an overnight etched in my mind memory of being stripped down to MY very core.

The same place I had yelled and screamed and coached clients to go harder, do more, is that all you got...became the same stomping ground for my dignity, my drive and my devil's voice crying I-can't-take much-more-I've-got-nothing-left inside.

128

Ironic.

Or foreshadowing.

Or reinventing and rebirthing.

A wipe out of everything from before that could never and never would be again.

A second death that smiled somewhere along the way knowing God was preparing me for a restoration NOT of things, but of beliefs.

The electric still got shut off.

At least half a dozen times.

And my cell phone was NOT always able to be paid on time. I can't even count how many times I had it reconnected and restarted and reset. The late fees and charges could have funded a vacation to Fiji and forget about the credit card payments. They were last on the list.

Even in our hope to start over, we couldn't keep up pace. Hope wasn't enough. You think eviction would erupt your eyes to calling it quits.

But not me.

I had already given up a home and things and cars and money and possessions and friends and even family.

For a Dream. For Faith. For Freedom. After all, I didn't come this far to come this far.

I wasn't going to stop until God said so. And All I heard from Him was keep going. *I have plans to prosper you and not harm you, do not be weary in doing good, keep running the race set out before you...*

BUT honestly, I think he may have pulled up a chair and was lounging back enjoying the shit show down below. Laughing at me making a bigger mess than before, yet always somehow untangling it in the nick of time.

I knew I could do this thing though.

I knew I could.

I knew, because when I was lying in that hospital bed with three tubes draining a deadly infection out of me, with part of my spine having just been urgently and in an emergency removed before death caught up to me, with legs not functioning and with my hope worn and weary, I made it out alive then.

Living in my gym...

Was a cakewalk.

I remember wanting and willing to give anything to be better, to be healed, to be home with my babies, to have full use of my body, to just be able to get out of bed.

I remembered the fight I had in me then and it was the same fighting mentality that was driving me to put my head down and rhino my way forward one more day for my dreams.

I never once thought I didn't have the fortitude to get through that time.

So, this time WOULD be no different in my mind.

Living there never being able to go home

Day after day

Night after night

After the last client left and we didn't have anywhere to go, I would cry.

But I never once thought we wouldn't make it out. I never once thought the end was nearing and I would have to stay stuck in my failure as a mom, as an entrepreneur, as a gym owner, as a woman with such determination and drive.

God rebuilt my resilience in that hospital room when I woke up to a second chance at a life.

He unsettled me.

He unstuck me.

And He moved me with the nudge of fatherly wisdom that reminded me and embedded in my mindset - not here, not now, not ever.

And He did it again in that eviction letter.

And in that gym that we got to call home.

And in that parking lot

He took down my last little bit of everything.

And rightfully so.

So, I stole my strength from that and tied it into this. I took pride in our gym home. I tucked the bed sheets neatly into the air mattresses and yoga mats. I made up my kids' single bed with their stuffed Care Bears and dinosaurs they loved to snuggle with so much. Then I went on to teach seven or eight high-energy-action-packed-make-it-happen-motivating fitness classes with a smile on my face, hope in my heart, grit in my bloodstream and covered completely in a filth I could not wipe clean.

Nothing in your life is an accident. Or a mistake.

It's a lesson of opportunity to create the character running through your bloodstream. It's taking advantage of your adversity, so you walk with authority through the storms trying to save you.

Resilience is a toughness.

Not just a bouncing back from, but an absorption of all your storms

all your sorrows

all your sufferings

all your sadness

and repurposing all of that for a power to fuel you forward into whatever you dream.

Now I was NOT born a fighter. My mother didn't birth a relentless resilient baby with blonde hair and war paint under her hazel eyes. I didn't come out loaded with a machete ready to whack down the weeds awaiting me in my future life.

I read Nancy Drew and Judy Blume, played with Barbie Dolls, and My Little Pony and raised hell on the occasional dirt mounds found in the new construction neighborhoods that me and my brothers played fort on.

I was built into one relentless resilient badass by chasing an imaginary love and seeking a spotlight from the shadows of everything that always seemed to come before me and against me. A now known perspective of urgency versus importance that I would later come to understand.

Now that badass-ness came with a price tag costing me a tireless unending work ethic and effort to outrun my own shadow and endure my own faith.

Its been tiring.

Its been a lot of showing up ugly

Showing up in pain

Showing up broke

Showing up in heartache

Showing up grieving

Showing up smothered in that unnecessary numbness that fucks with your mind because it's all the feels all at once.

My resilience came from showing up THAT ugly.

Perfectly presenting a pseudo performance that she's got it all together in happiness and love and success. YET, every single second of the day, a great work was undergoing a tremendous transformation inside of me.

In spite of anything and everything, it is being the duck, swimming smoothly and serenely on the surface and pedaling its little orange feet powerfully underneath often times against the current.

It's setting up your homelessness into the best-roof-over-your-head home you can.

Resilient people show up ugly because we remember what is in our confidence arsenal from all the previous blows to our ego and self-acceptance and self-esteem and selflessness.

We work and rise from a place of victory, expecting to win and to overcome and to rise again. We do not expect defeat or accept it when it tries to break down the door. That, in fact, increases our rate at which we fight back even more so - as it becomes our fuel and fire as we press on in a fierce unrelenting pursuit for better.

We work in our wait, staying steadfast to our faith that it worked out once before, so therefore, IT WILL work itself out again. We don't care about the opinions of others, only the judgment of our future self and what we are and aren't leaving behind.

And rather than blaming all the worldly responsibilities we think we have, responsibilities that are commonplace to you and me and are so wickedly NOT unique, we go out and machete higher standards while onlookers call us high maintenance, crazy outrageous dreamers. YET they continue to wake up in Bill

Murrays *Groundhog Day*, repeating a numbness that dries up their dreams.

Meanwhile us crazy ones, wild ones, free spirit ones, rule breakers, risk takers, adventuring irresponsible ones CREATE a newness that was never before BY choosing to cancel out any chaos controlling inconsistencies that try to stifle our commitments to being better.

Our excuses and explanations are no different than yours, but we don't resign to them. We just Go. We get in front of it. And then, in what seems like one giant whack, but is actually the sum of every single swing in the past, We Goliath it.

What heaviness on your heart do you feel? What would you be willing to go homeless for? What crazy dreams inside of you are screaming get me out? What hurts, what pains, what past of yours has created a song inside of you that brings tears and chokes your ability to forget the hurt that it caused you? What resilience is inside you that has helped you? What has built you? What choices have you made that led you astray? What choices have led you further along? What dreams are you willing to step up and sacrifice for? What life are you living that your kids would look at you and say, Hell Yeah Mom/Dad? Would you want them to model their life after yours? Would you sleep on a floor for your faith? Can you rise now in your aftermath? Will you choose resilience, or will you choose the reasons why you stay the same?

Robyn McLeod Thrasher

pieces

A Flashback of Your Faithful Fights

An Arduous Picking up of Your Past

Pain and Pleasures

The Art of Collecting Memories that

Mold You Mercilessly

A Knowing Their Slivers Still Soothe You

your **befores**

it comes in many forms, wearing many costumes and interchangeable masks

When I first think of resilience and adversity, Rocky is one of the first characters that comes to mind.

He is an iconic silver screen legend that embodies these elements. Not just for his boxing skills and talent, but for his attitude and ability to get back up blow after blow – inside and outside of the ring.

"It aint about how hard you get you hit. It's about how hard you can get hit and keep moving forward."

The story alone of how Sylvester Stallone wrote, pitched and sold his Rocky story is beyond the epitome of rising into resilience.

Back in the early 70's when Sylvester Stallone was an unknown actor trying to make a way. He was struggling, broke and reluctantly had to sell his dog because he wasn't sure he could afford to feed him. One night after seeing Muhammad Ali fight, Sylvester went home inspired, alive in creativity, and in three days wrote the script of Rocky.

At his next audition, he was passed over but mentioned his "Rocky" movie to the producers. A few days later they offered him six figures for the rights but didn't want Sylvester playing the lead role. He was a "nobody" and they wanted a "somebody."

Now somehow, he knew in his gut he had to be the one to play the lead role of Rocky. He contemplated passing up the money as he was accustomed to living in his poverty.

But after negotiating with the producers, they eventually gave him the lead role, a million dollars and kept the film under budget by using handheld cameras and family and friends to make his dream a legend on the big screen.

Call it a stretch, but he listened to his screams.

He knew he had more.

He knew he had something special. And he wasn't willing to settle for it.

We all know how the story turns out.

He made movie history.

But did you know, he got his dog back?!

NOW, we aren't all stepping into the ring to get pummeled by Apollo Creed but day-by-day, hour-by-hour we're all dodging hits or taking punches in the ring of life.

So, what is adversity exactly?

Because it comes in many forms, wearing many costumes and interchangeable masks. The worst kind often comes in the dark when we can't see it coming, it's that sucker punch silently sneaking up on us so much so that our first glance is a blur of a beast, and we fail to realize it for the giant it can become.

According to Google, adversity is simply defined as difficult times.

What the hell?

Difficult times?

That's a little broad don't you think?

Let's break that down. Because what you think is difficult ...burpee box jump overs and double dumbbell thrusters, I think is easy.

And what I think is difficult... navigating anything technology and putting shit together, excel spreadsheets and driving outside my five-mile radius in bumper-to-bumper traffic, you might be able to do with your eyes closed upside down and backwards.

It's easy to judge someone when you think your filth is dirtier than theirs. Harder than theirs. You got the short end of the stick, you think, but let's leave the judgment to the big guy upstairs.

My point is: My pain is no less or no more than your pain. Your adversity is just that because you see it as so. And mine is mine, even IF you can't see the brutality behind it.

So, since we are defining adversity, let's play a little game.

That means it's interactive time again.

Yay!

Go get a highlighter.

I mean you should already have one by now because you're highlighting the you know what out of all the nuggets in this book. But just in case you don't, take a second to go grab one.

.

.

.

OK, so now that you are prepared, I'm going to start listing "Adversities" and "Difficult Times." I want you to highlight all the ones that have affected you or attacked you in some way.

OK?

Ready?

Set?

Go!

Loss of a Parent

Loss of a Child

Near-Death Experience – For Yourself.

Now not like not some stupid childhood bike riding accident when you ran into the parked white van and flipped off your handlebars near-death experience (that wasn't me at all multiple times with the same white van in the same parked place while on the same pink banana seat bicycle).

No, I mean, a life and death experience where you should not be here today reading this book highlighting these words experience.

Like hooked up to machines to keep you ticking experience

On chemo

On ventilators

Sepsis shutting down slowly experience

In an actual real life hazmat suits quarantine like death experience

Defibrillator brought back to life

That kind of near-death experience.

Now what about:

Chronic illness

Mental health illness or issues

An injury that left you disabled or disgruntled

A car accident caused by you

A car accident not caused by you

A sports accident trauma

What about war

And divorce

An affair on either end of that shitty stick?

And then there is addiction.

Addiction to anything

Drugs

Alcohol

Smoking

Vaping

Food

Sex

Spending money you don't have

Gambling

Your job

More money

Or

Enabling an Addict

Even loving an addict is an addictive adversity in itself.

What about

Poverty

Bankruptcy

Financial loss

Financial ruin

Waking up to an empty bank account NOT by your own accord

Waking up to an empty bank account by YOUR own accord

Hiding from creditors

Past due bills piling up

Have you had your utilities cut off not because you forgot to pay the bill but because you Could NOT pay the bills?

Eviction

Repossessed cars

Repossessed things

Piggy bank days?

Homelessness for any period of time (living with your parents while you are in between building houses does NOT count)

If you've ever had to sleep on the floor for 1, 2, 3, 4, 5, 6 months or more highlight this motherclucker.

If you ever had to scrouge around the house to find things to sell things to buy a carton of eggs and loaf of bread at the grocery store, go ahead and highlight and double star both sides here.

OR maybe you've had to stand in line at the food pantry with your pride on the floor and your head held down low as they handed you the brown sack with groceries inside.

How's the highlighting going?

Have you ever gotten laid off?

Been fired?

Passed up when you knew you were the right one for the job, but they gave it to someone else anyways?

Ever been betrayed?

What about abused?

Maybe you were the abuser

Maybe you were the receiver

Physically

Verbally

Emotionally

Sexually

Mentally

Ever been spit on?

Hit

Punched

Choked

Raped

Or faced the awfulness of abortion

Ever suffered a miscarriage

Battled infertility

I know I'm getting into some tough stuff here.

So how many have you highlighted?

As you can see, difficult times is so loosely defined, right?

It's comical. But as I have said, Adversity is all among us and everybody gets a dose. Sometimes a double. Often because we're the ones trying break free of generational and self-induced curses - swinging our machetes like welcome signs - waving the BS over our way and then flipping our middle finger up when it finally walks in and says Hey!

I mean, what were we expecting?

Resilient people are the fighters living to make a dent in some kind of worldly difference. We are being called upon to stand at the front of the line - dirty and determined. We aren't playing it safe snuggling under the covers or middle of the pack - packing it.

We are in full blown open season, standing with our arms open wide, chin up, chest proud shoulders back and down, KNOWING it's not a possibility that we might get hurt or burned or beat down in the process, but it's a SURE fucking thing.

Adversity is not a down on your luck day that passes quietly into the night. In fact, I think adversity is a horrific thunderstorm meant to disrupt our lives intentionally and purposely on purpose.

I think it is meant to almost nearly devastate us... BUT stops just shy of a complete and total demolition, so that we are forced to think WTF, why is this storm coming for me? What is it trying to tell me, teach me, give me?

I think Adversity wants us to breakdown, so we can build back up, only better. Like thunder striking in the middle of the night, it's meant to jolt us awake, open our eyes and clear out all the BS, so we can see ourselves on the silver screen BUT in real life and FOR who and what we really are.

These "adversities" are tough. They take courage to come out of. And hell, I'm sure I've missed a few, so feel free to write in your own right here on this page.

BS that has happened to me that she missed:

You're welcome.

Here's THE THING: not everybody makes it through. Some just can't handle the renovation required to rise after the debris has settled in. The disruption IT (adversity) brings is an overwhelming occupation, overpowering many and saving so few. AND THAT is where you have to ask yourself, is this YOU? Are you settled in the debris or are you wiping that shit off?

Adversity affects us all, but some of us have left the building while many of YOU are still lingering in the dust of what's left in the rubble.

You KNOW you need to get the fuck out, but You are still living in it, sitting in it, breathing in it. In fact, you are bathing in the filth of it.

Of how it USED to be

Before...

of how it WAS supposed to be

Before...

of WHAT it used to be

Before...

I hate to break the news to you, BUT BEFORE packed its bags and is long gone AND She ain't ever coming back.

So, what you went through...

how mad you were...

how mad you still are...

how pissed off you feel...

how hurt your heart cries inside...

how stunned your ego got stung...

It ain't ever going back. There is no reverse button to rewind you back to BEFORE it all happened.

BEFORE I got sick, my stepmom was healthy, and I had my best friend and my person to call every day.

BEFORE I got sick, I lived in a happy looking house with happy looking pictures and a happy family of four plus a happy little dog and a happy little grey cat that both my kids carried around all very happily.

BEFORE I got sick, I could walk without a limp or sticky gait. I could lift barbells above my head and box on heavy bags without resentment.

BEFORE I got sick, I could sit and stand without getting stuck.

BEFORE I got sick, I didn't have anxiety about healthcare and doctors that brushed me aside and stole my trust in their tests and scientific machines that were supposed to catch the sickness that seeped inside of me.

BEFORE I got sick, I had no chronic pain ailing me hourly.

BEFORE I got sick, I had no complications complicating my character.

BEFORE I got sick, I didn't know the difference between a crippling mindset and a convicted one.

BEFORE, I got sick, I smiled without a story to define it.

BEFORE I got sick, I didn't know the REAL me.

BUT YOU...

ALL you are STILL seeing is what you HAD

What you lost

What you miss

What you used to belong to

What you used to believe in

YOU don't see WHY the Disruption came specifically for you. SO, you whine and complain and whimper in the weight of their leftovers and I hate to tell you, but I'm going to anyway:

it's why you're overweight

it's why you're lazy

it's why you're depressed

it's why you're anxious

it's why you're sad

it's why you're broke

it's why you're posturing happiness

it's why all your picture posting on social media are shams

it's why you scroll all day long

it's why you can't focus

it's why you don't have any energy to do anything at all

it's why you don't have any faith

its why you don't have any fight

and I get it

I am not judging you

I have been there

I was you

In fact, I've highlighted almost that entire list back there.

BEFORE, I was living a lie.

BEFORE, I was living in a contempt of faithfulness to myself and to those I once loved.

BEFORE, I was surrounded by people, but never felt more alone.

BEFORE, I let my body be used in an exchange of hoping for a little taste of love.

BEFORE, I wasn't making a difference to others, I was just so overly self-consumed in my counterfeit world of how it could ONLY help me.

BEFORE, I was lost looking in my bathroom mirror staring sickly into the deep space between what was and what has come to BE.

So, yeah, fuck the adversities.

The difficulties.

The disruptions.

The BS.

Fuck you BS.

And Fuck me too.

It blows.

BUT the bottom line. Adversity sucks and difficult is difficult. It's like walking around with your very own Linus from Charlie Brown as your personal filth cloud following you everywhere you go.

So, what do WE (and when I say We I mean YOU) do now?

Well, for starters, look at all that highlighted BS that was ONCE your life. How do we flip the mindset switch when we are still sneering at the words on a page as they compete in a staring contest for your future success?

How do we shift our attitude about it all?

The trauma

The turmoil

The tension

The torture

And how do we develop tenacity to endure because this shit is hard?

How do we stop ourselves from getting stuck?

And how do we unstuck ourselves when we suddenly see our feet sinking in the quicksand and don't have a rope to pull us out?

How do we keep going while we are in the process of hurting, but hunger for healing?

In the coaching I've done over the course of 26 years, the most common choice in almost all of my clients (I would put money on this) was their crazy ass commitment to choosing to suffer in it.

I wanted to bang my head against the wall as I watched them sacrifice what COULD BE to settling and succumbing and staying put and stagnant in their own BS of Before.

Again and again, they would go to back choosing what was killing them, not even softly, BUT screaming ever so loudly. AND rather than press the big red easy button for better, I've watched them press the pause button on their life so hard that even that got stuck.

Life happened one too many times to you.

And I AM sorry.

I am.

It sucks.

I know.

But staying small and shrinking, hiding in the hope of your one days, should haves and I wish I could haves, takes much more energy mentally, physically, emotionally, and spiritually than it will ever take for you to give your BEFORES a second glance and say good-effing bye.

Adios.

Peace out.

BUT

Maybe

Just maybe that **Near-Death Experience** gave you a new reverence for life. The ability to appreciate every day. To Be Present. **To Be Here Now**. To add a priority tag to the purpose you were meant for more. I know one of my lessons from my almost dying is an upmost **Urgency** for life. Like foot on the gas pedal, tomorrow isn't promised, so let's go for it all today.

And that **Divorce** you went through but didn't ask for…WERE you really happy anyway? Maybe this is your second chance to start a new relationship with yourself, set new standards, pay more attention, become a better partner, listen attentively, hold hands, kiss goodnight and run the dishwasher every once in awhile.

Bankruptcy: So, you sucked with money. You overspent. You got carried away. You were irresponsible. Probably a little greedy too, wouldn't you say? Now you have an opportunity to master money management. To save. To pay in cash. To rebuild your reputation by making responsible decisions. Maybe you work smarter to achieve independence from relying on borrowed choices.

Eviction/Repossession: So, you lost it all. So, what. Now you've learned to live with less. AND actually appreciate things because you know what's it like to do without and to go without. You know what it's like leave the material stuff of this world behind and understand the VALUE that they really hold IS no value at all. You'll buy less and spend more where it really matters. Quality time. Love. Adventure. Attention. Serving. Giving. Doing.

Got Fired or Lost your Job: Could that be the universe nudging you to jump into that business you always felt called to do? Or start showing up for your family because you had been wasting away at a job you didn't like anyways? Maybe it's time to go back to school. Get the degree or serve in your community. Write the book. Go on the audition. Fuck. Just walk the damn dog without the rat race running you ragged in a resentful routine.

Illness: You do NOT have a full complete knowledge of what it is to be 1000% appreciative of your body until it is stolen from you. Your illness awakens you to the delicacy of life and the importance of living in good health with an able body. Maybe this illness will have you eating whole foods instead of gorging on fast foods. Maybe this illness will have you moving more, walking and running towards your fight for THE right life. Maybe this illness or that sickness brought you closer to the urgency of living alive.

Abuse: As horrific and as heartbreaking as it is, it can bring about a new understanding of what love is and what love isn't. Abuse displays your demons and shows you your standards. What you allow. What you are capable of and who you do NOT want to be. Abuse calls out parts of you that you didn't know existed and never want to meet again. Abuse can give you an endurance and an unstoppable willpower for freedom in your life. And it can and will sink its teeth in so deeply that your soul suffers NO MORE needlessly.

Addiction: Gives you the gift of validation that something inside of you is a fighting to be free. It's a gigantic flashing red light signaling you to stop pushing your shit away - to own it, to release it, to honor your pain, heal your hurt and seek a better way than fending off your feelings with a fast fix that is never filling. While addiction defends your neediness and emptiness inside, IF you seek you shall see it also reveals your lack of, and want of, and your deeper desire to answer your true screams. It shows you what you are missing. You just need to tap into the dark hole it is digging inside of you.

YOUR difficult times are beautiful disasters if you are willing to drop the defensive lines and open your eyes to it. They can be found ONLY after the disruptions that came for you are finally told goodbye.

Your adversities CAN become your adventures. You can retell them as stories of what happened BEFORE, but more importantly of WHO they helped you BECOME.

Resilient people Do. Not. Suffer.

Remember, suffering is settling, and We DON'T settle.

We hurt. We have pain. But we do not volunteer to be victims.

We move with an urgency, like the swiftness that comes with the crashing of waves, never ceasing to see how far behind BEFORE is.

WE, resilient people, look ahead, step firmly towards the deep end without fighting the waters coming crashing at our heads. We let the waters wash over us and cleanse our filth away from deep within.

Take a look back at your Difficult Times highlights. What BEFORES can you recall here? What BEFORE story do you continuously tell stories about? How can you flip it? How can you edit the outcome to showcase the good rather than stay hung up on the bad? Everyone loves a good comeback story, so go rewrite your own version of Rocky. Unless of course, you want to choose to stay the same.

You can disagree with my responses and reactions and rebuttals to handling adversities OR you can choose a choice to find the goodness in those disruptions that came not just to make you bleed, but to make YOU believe.

endurance

A Longing of Toleration

An Unending Steadiness

The Art of Withstanding Difficulty

A Knowing of Never Quitting

mama bear

when my hope and my faith and my grit
and my strength had expired... and it
had... my endurance endured with me

Endurance is the secret weapon you've been waiting for.

Without it you cannot fully emerge through anything and last. You WILL settle
back in your old BS, all your old BEFORES, your adversities and your difficulties.
Resilience will NEVER walk in the door to meet you if you can't endure the
journey to greet it.

But remember,

WE *insert hand clap emoji here in your mind*

ARE *and here*

NOT *and here*

SETTLING.

Not

Any

More!

Endurance is the American Idol It Factor to winning whatever you are battling. It IS the Navy Seal Special Ops Badass yanking your ass up out the shallow end while the white caps keep crashing over your head when you're already knocked down.

Without Endurance, overcoming adversity is like trying to breathe without oxygen. You will gasp for air in all the wrong places and eventually YOU WILL give up.

I'm going to give you a movie trailer teaser about me crawling on the floor and about how it built my endurance to endure one of the most excruciating sanctifications I've ever endured.

I was about to begin the fight of my life without training, without practice and without any count down or any warning. Hell, I didn't even get to sign up for the event that would come to knockout my life. There was certainly no carb loading and I didn't have time put on my "pump up song" to warm up either.

I was just called up.

He said Fight.

And so, I did.

For months, my body had been deteriorating very slowly and very quietly. Only I could feel the screams inside and feel their hands clenching down on me. This disruption, with my nametag written in big bold CAPS, had come with one motive, to KILL the lies and save the soul inside.

I was dying from the inside out.

Invisible to almost everyone but myself and my God.

When they saw me crawling on the floor, they didn't see what was inside of me, swirling in a storm of its own rage from living a lie and dying from the disease of it.

They saw an otherwise healthy woman, with no outward signs of distress and yelled at me to get up and walk. They couldn't see the disruption that had come for me.

They saw a weakling and a wimp. A joke to laugh, tease and taunt at. They saw me milking it and making excuses to not get up from it.

They could not see the diseases eating away at me.

ONE, a wildly rare infectious illness that was seeping through my blood, bones, muscles and organs

AND

TWO, the deadly disease of deceit and depression and desperation for a stopping of the lies leeching onto my soul.

I'm going to tell you about me NOT being able to tie my own shoes, put on my pants or even get up out of bed on my own. I'm going to tell you about strangers helping me go to the bathroom in a wheelchair like port-a-potty at my bedside in a very un-private like hospital room.

My dignity stripped down to its most naked state.

I'm going to tell you about tubes that cut into me to draw out a deadly bacterium seeping through my vanity and my veins. I'm going to tell you about how I was left to advocate for my own body, and for my own health and for my own mental state with more than nine doctors, two hospital weeklong stays, ambulances rides threefold and an unbelievable amount of morphine to mask the madness they couldn't see thriving on the inside of me.

I'm going to tell you about big machines and their inconclusive tests. Nurses that

163

judged me. And nurses that loved me. Doctors that dismissed me. Doctors that eye-rolled me. Doctors that didn't even look up from their clipboards at me.

I'm going to tell you about test after test after test result coming up supposedly clean and clear. I'm going to tell you about the I should go home and soak my feet in hot water and let my hormones rest without fear.

I'm going to tell you that they said it was alright - YET all the wrongs built upon more wrongs and those wrongs built upon more wrongs eventually built a monumental mistake that sent me home to die with both my diseases still trapped inside.

I'm going to tell you that I was called to fight AND so I kept fighting for me. That I didn't know what or why, BUT I knew there was more that I had to do.

Another phone call. Another doctor. Another test. Another cry for help. The screams inside me weren't letting up. They were on a ceaseless repeat.

I'm going to tell you about a real quarantine. One with no visitors and yellow hazmat suits. A time after the mistakes had finally made their way out, I was suddenly a delicate science project that needed protection in my unsteady state.

I'm going to tell you about the ICU nurse who remained with me through a long hard arduous night. Waiting for me to slumber into my pain, she sat with me sharing pictures of her teenage son. Her smile still bright in my memories.

I'm going to tell you about the woman who prayed for me when I didn't believe in God. That asked for my permission to speak words of His healing over me as she stood at my bedside crying out to Him for His grace and His mercy.

I'm going to tell you about "Sad Eyes" who saved me the minute I saw him walk in the room and sit down next to me. Holding my hand and gently squeezing as he revealed that death was coming directly for me.

And I'm going to tell you about the screams that died inside of me when the surgeons swindled me out of MY choice to choose my own adventure story.

When I didn't get a say.

When my choice was death or emergency spine surgery and possibly paralyzation – WE would just have to wait and see.

When my choice was really - PLEASE just save me.

I'm going to tell you about the first steps I fought for after waking up into my new life with no closure on the old one BEFORE. With new legs that were unworkable in the moment they forced me to get up and get moving forward. Just a step they said. And then I was back down in that bed.

I'm going to tell you about living lethargic with medicine for months that may or may not have kept me alive. A crapshoot of medical cocktails thrust in my arm through a tube taking the drugs straight to my once healthy heart.

I'm going to tell you that I had to administer it all to my own damn self, twice a day for three months and a little more, while I struggled up hardwood steps to the second floor to kiss my daughter and my son goodnight.

They were just babies at the time. Then five and three. I convinced myself they needed me to tuck them in to sleep. BUT looking back, now I know, it was me who needed their embrace so desperately.

I'm going to tell you that it is STILL taking me time to recover from this BEFORE. Eight years later it still gets to me THAT I never got to grieve the life I lost BEFORE. There was no goodbye, no closure, no wait a minute and just one more thing. And while it sounds silly because my old life was killing me, I hungered to see it JUST one more time. Just to tell it, I told you so, now fuck off and thank you all at the same time.

All THAT

Brought upon my ability to get the fuck up and make a way out. I didn't know the severity of it all, but I felt the strength of the screams shouting at me

Don't YOU quit.

My endurance emerged no doubt. It rescued me. It saved me. It built me back better.

Fighting with doctors

Fighting with medicines

Fighting with tests that didn't tell the whole truth

Fighting with family

Fighting with the pain wrapped around and all inside of me - crawling up through my spine and to my brain, lodged in my joints and secretly conjuring up an all-out war inside of me.

This was BEYOND tiring. When my hope and my faith and my grit and my strength had expired. AND it had. My endurance endured with me.

Though I live in pain today, constant and incessant and as relentless as me, I am no baby, so I use it to fuel me every damn day.

Every run.

Every squat.

Every lunge.

Every punch on the heavy bag.

It empowers me to keep seeing what I see.

Every word I type.

Every hope I write.

Every dream I see.

Endurance keeps me living for what my FAITH says is waiting for me.

When this happened to me, I looked normal on the outside, but I was truly rotting away. It was an intense invisible pain that was idling inside of me, stirring up so much more than just the hard to pronounce infection that had come for me.

My body has been beach body perfect. It has been physique-building-trophy-winning-stage-ready. It has been super skinny from hours on a stair mill and 43 pounds too heavy from filling it with *Dunkin Donuts* and one too many treats that I was unable to put down at will.

It has birthed two babies. Ran multiple marathons, a Tough Mudder and some crazy ass military bootcamp obstacle course run where they hurl you over 12 feet walls. It has survived eight surgeries in all, a Rottweiler dog attack and a Mexican moped accident that still makes my second dad's skin crawl.

It has worked out since it was 15 consistently, naturally and organically making friends with all the weights and exercise machines that drew it in. It has been a dancer, a cheerleader, and an aerobics instructor. A boxer, a trainer, and a really horrible tennis player. It has scuba dived, cliff jumped, climbed some really beautiful mountain tops and wandered in cities with bright neon city lights.

It's tough, tenacious and holds its pain in a place of very high tolerance. THEN and now, I appear as normal as anyone else can be. Yet, my bones and muscles and all their interlocking connecting pieces NOW share space with a laundry list of medical jargon I cannot even speak.

There is no recovery for me. There is just manageability of the aftermath that my missing pieces now bring.

They removed part of my spine and IT is all very twisted and achy and STILL very angry at me. My hips are jacked up. My leg is mostly numb. I've got one leg that's all Tiggerish with his hoo-hoo-hoo-hooing. While the other one is Eeyore moving aimlessly in self-pity. It's a chore to get them to step in line, yet we always find a way to bounce and skip or drag and push our way through together depending on the day.

Eight years later, I am still enduring the disruption that came to claim me. I downplay it because it's not a visible deformity. I downplay it because I lived, kept my legs and got to learn to walk again. I downplay it because I compare myself to others who outwardly look like their disruption was way worse than the one that came for me.

Now I know, THIS is not the truth, but it is the mindfuck that diminishes what it LEFT me with, what it took FROM me and what it GAVE me as it redefined me.

The pain it brought me is ghostly and I don't think it will ever go away. Physically or mentally. Emotionally or spiritually. I've just learned to live with it better. I've learned the limits it gave me. I've learned the grace in God's goodness for keeping me. I've learned that moving is the medicine that serves me best - SO - embracing its residence is what I am left wrestling with.

Maybe for you it's an addiction or a secret sin. Maybe it's shame from past choices and grace you just haven't been given. Maybe it's anxiety or as simple and as sad as you are wishing away the days that you have been adorned with. Maybe it's the loss of a loved one, a crushed dream or a medical ailment like me. Whatever IT is for you, IT is most likely invisible to the rest of us to see.

So, as we stand there watching you on your hamster wheel of life, LISTEN to the whisper telling you to crawl on the hard cold floor and start pushing yourself but pacing yourself because it is NOT in your consistency or grit or book smarts that will get you to where you want to be. IT is your ability to ENDURE everything in your path on your way there.

It won't even be your brave boldness that will get you across that finish line. Those things didn't help get me through months of physical therapy and administering my own medicine. They didn't push me mentally as I learned to take first steps again. They didn't get me through a divorce and eviction and homelessness.

My ability to endure it all DID because I outlasted the pain as it was passing.

You see, IF you stay in the battle long enough, you'll know it's all just a big coming and going. And the only way to beat it IS to endure it as it flows however fast or however slow it seeps through your path.

Consistency and Grit and Determination and Wisdom are top players, don't get me wrong. But Endurance is your Queen. These other guys are your army. Your backup. Your ride or die. But Endurance, she's your Mama Bear. Brazen, brave, on alert and expectant, patient to outlast and protect her pack. She's Strong. Mighty. And fierce for a fight. She won't let you back down IF you can build her up along this life.

It is in YOUR ability to keep going. To withstand. To take another step. To get back up.

To EVEN go slow, but to effing go. To be tireless in your effort when enduring the setbacks and the sadness and the suffering and the sorrow and the silence that comes to steal your strength and your smiles seem like they are setting up permanency.

ALL of that will eventually end as you endure it. If you keep your head up and you keep going. You must remain steady. You MUST declare, I WILL NEVER GIVE UP. I will never concede.

Unfortunately, MOST people do. They just quit too soon. And we are all guilty of it at one time or another. Perplexed at the roadblocks or dead ends that we faced, stuck at the fork in the road, paralyzed by indecision and the fatigue that hardship doesn't gift wrap for you.

We get weary and worn out and unable to reach and release the resilience inside. Waking up one day seeing only the impossibilities and issues that have isolated us into a stuckness and a settlement built on suffering. What a shithole that is.

Consistency gets you on a schedule. Grit will have you rolling up your sleeves. Determination gets you knee deep in the dirt. Wisdom shouts out your next steps. BUT Endurance commands you to keep going. To keep whacking and whacking and whacking and when you ask how much more, IT LIES, so you never know when to stop. You just go and go and go and go until your going never needs to stop.

We can all commit. We can all be consistent. We can all have courage. We can all take chances.

BUT if you can't take it, YOU can't make it.

So be the first one kneeling and the last one standing. Always be looking for a way. Making a way and taking machetes to anything that stands up and tries to get in your way.

Be a renegade. Be a leader. Take the hits. Then keep moving. Keep believing. Keep trying. Keep starting over. Even if it is back to the back of the line.

Endure like a Mama Bear in the grizzly winter woods. Give up for nothing and for no one.

What limits have you put on your endurance? When have you stopped short in life? What would happen if you kept going? What would happen if you did one more of anything? Do you find yourself starting over again and again on the same path because WHY...you gave up one day, one hour, one minute too soon? Can you recall life happens moments in your life that you thought you would never make it through, YET here you are? What did you do then? What made that doable but not THIS?

Check your mindset on endurance. Are you really done OR can you keep pushing further and further and further until you've made it to a clearing on the other side of the war within?

application

A Following Through on Your Consumption

An Execution of Your Promises

The Art of Doing

A Knowing of Exhausting All Efforts

Robyn McLeod Thrasher

mindset **midpoint**

you choose your choices... so, make
sure your adventures are your own

Don't be that person that reads and highlights and puts the book back on the shelf forever forgetting to apply and implement your Machete Mentality. Take notes now. Do a book report now. I've even made it easy and created a cheat sheet for you. So PLEASE, re-read and refresh and remind your mindset NOW, so it remembers how to stay relentless as you continue your journey whacking through your unbeaten path.

- The WAY out is always THROUGH. So don't stop whacking until you make a way that clears space for your soul to soak in all the strength that is meant for you.

- The filthy four-letter words you need to be on guard for are L-I-E-S and all your B-U-T-S's keeping you restrained. Keep it up and I'm sure my mom still has a bar of Ivory Soap she can lend you to cleanse yourself of those should be curse words.

- And your FILTH doesn't have to be totally wiped clean before you walk through the threshold of His house. In fact, He encourages the welcoming of your little bits and pieces of lodged in dirt and grime that coat your flesh exposing your faith and fortitude from every single fight.

- Give yourself a Kevin Hart pat on the back more often than not. Those small wins are step ups and ins that help you climb and maintain as you ascend through all of your life happens adversities.

- You CHOOSE your choices. So, MAKE sure YOUR adventures are your own.

- QUIT getting back in line. Stay Steady. Stay Strong. Stay focused forward. YOU are ALMOST there. I know you can't see it, but I can. Trust the Process. It WILL prevail.

- Your BS is – are – your bad stories you've been telling yourself to excuse you from showing up in THIS life. STOP that and START standing up to the bully inside your head.

- The whisper quietly urging you to go, to move, to do, to jump IS a muffled SCREAM coming from the depths of your life trapped inside and it's desperately seeking its permanent release. Let it Go to let it be Free.

- STUCK and SETTLED are lazy liars tempting you to stay complacent and compliant with a life lesser than of all you are capable of being.

- And all that wondering back to what it was like BEFORE is irreversible irrelevant time. BEFORE has packed her bags and She isn't coming back for you. So, stop living in the memories of her shadow that are stunting your more than settling second-best personality.

- Endurance is the insatiable Mama Bear you NEED. So, let her pace you or you will find yourself quitting your journey just a few short steps shy of greeting the life waiting on your ability to withstand the deep.

My HOPE is to pull all the potential out of you. AND to expose an exchange in you that eliminates the temptation to stay stuck in what happened to you AND awaken the fighter in you to start whacking and whacking and whacking again.

fight

A War for More

An Indomitable Spirit for Success

The Art of Calling Your Shots

A Knowing in Standing up For Your Truth

get the F-up

getting up is the one thing you can control - that you can choose to do

First things First.

Multiple curse word alert.

Enduring doesn't mean crying at rock bottom and waiting for the storm to blow over.

So, let's go ahead and get up.

Yes, YOU.

GET.

THE.

FUCK.

UP.

It happened.

So, what.

Life happens.

Get the fuck up and quit thinking YOU are so special that YOU are the only one IT is happening to.

Spoiler alert.

You ARE Special, BUT not THAT Special.

Life Happens.

Again

and again

and again

and again.

And IT is happening to each and every one of us.

Right now.

We aren't alone in our battles. Remember all those highlights a few chapters ago? You weren't the only one highlighting up this book.

Adversity is among ALL of us. It is Everywhere.

Exposed AND expertly hidden like the golden egg at Easter.

Learning to walk in that, is actually a simple process and I've laid it all out for you right here,

BUT FIRST You GOTTA Get the F@#! Up.

You gotta move.

You gotta move your body and you gotta move your mind.

Like your life depends on it.

Because it does.

Do Not try to figure out WHY it happened. Not right now. Don't sit in it. Don't suffer in it.

MOVE from it. The faster the better. Physically & psychologically. MOVE.

Now I won't go into the science behind it because honestly, I don't care WHY something works the way it works. I just want to TRUST that if I do it or use it, IT WILL get me to where I want to go. And believe me, I've been through enough to know MOVING works.

Statistics and studies and charts and graphs and reports with lots of numbers show me what everybody else did or didn't do. BUT MOVING, shows me what I can do personally to pull my ass up from where I am at RIGHT NOW, in my crappy moment of I don't want to, I don't feel like it, AND it will put me in a new place that re-directs me into a more positive position of HELL YES, let's do this, I got this.

Without overthinking and over-analyzing and over-processing. Without the planning and prepping and procrastinating over which "study" to follow... I just follow the one that gets me into a new mental state. A new emotional state. A new spiritual state. And obviously a new physical state.

Sometimes, most times, YOU just need to DO. To apply. To execute. To effing MOVE.

I can tell you MOVING is undoubtedly proven to change your state of mind. Fact check me. GO ahead. Google will tell you the same damn thing.

Do more doing.

Less talking.

Less planning.

Less prepping.

Just simply more doing.

So, if you're sitting in your BS, GET up and get MOVING.

It will immediately alter the state of your mentality, your emotions, your mood, your self-esteem, your joy, your peace, your effing freedom from all the BS you are trying to stay sitting in for whatever reason.

Stop that.

Get out of bed.

Get off the couch.

Get off your phone.

Stop scrolling.

Stop crying.

Stop complaining.

Stop excusing.

Stop hoping.

Stop wishing.

Stop obsessing.

Stop planning.

Just stop it. *Insert hand clapping emoji here.* You know what? *Go ahead and make it three times for emphasis please!*

And START moving.

I guarantee YOU - you will feel better.

It won't solve the problem, the root, the reason, the why, BUT it will alleviate the symptoms. It will give you relief to breathe again, to focus, to see clearer, to feel calmer, to be more forgiving with yourself, more forgiving with others, to be more deliberate, to be more intense with your effort.

Getting up IS the one thing you CAN control - THAT you CAN choose to do.

It doesn't have to be crazy back flips through tires with a sprint to the finish line, it just needs to be something that REMOVES you from your current psychological shitty state of feeling sorry for yourself and suffering in your own settlement of accepting less than the best of yourself AND MOVING you physically towards the pursuit of something better off in the distance that with time and endurance and all its ride-or-die soldiers will resurrect the YOU inside of YOU that doesn't give up.

SO, MOVE!

Now, the second part to this moving is becoming aware of how long you were down. How long it took you to get up. How long it took you to get moving again. How long it festered inside. How long you fought it. Resisted and rebelled against you.

Take a note.

An hour

A day

A week

A month

A year????

As you grow in building your resiliency rate, the speed at which you train yourself to MOVE, to get up faster WILL increase. And the downtime at which you are anchored in your adversity will decrease.

I promise.

But YOU must be willing to walk away from the IT dragging you back down the rabbit hole of defeat and DO so without looking back.

What is something that gets you stuck? What circumstance GETS you? Grabs you? Pulls you down. Mentally and emotionally gut punches you again and again and again?

Is there a pattern?

What is your kryptonite? What is your Achilles heel?

WHY do you think that is? Is it coming from an old experience? Is it coming from now? Is it TRUE? Or are you making up stories in your head? Do you have actual facts that have brought you to this stuck state of sitting in your own mess or someone else's? What would it take for you to get up faster? What would PULL you out of it? How have you done it in the past? YOU see all my 5W's & H at work here, right?

Use them. They work.

feelings

A Rush of Everything and Nothing All at Once

An Overwhelming Cleansing of the Soul

The Art of Understanding Your Voids

A Knowing that Runs Rampant

Through Your Bones

meet **turbo**

he is a fiery combination of all
my unresolved fierce feelings
totally unsatiable, unstoppable

Enduring the BS gets you through IT, and therefore builds your
I-can-take-anything-thermometer.

BUT what happens when you get to the other side of IT? How do you see it
coming again? Prevent it? Be proactive about it? How do you even know what IT
is? How can you build up your ability to endure IT much like your resiliency rate?

Easy.

You bring about awareness and acknowledgment to whatever IT is. You give it
some space to speak. To breathe.

You feel it. You get all BFF with it. Keep it close. And get friendlier and cozier
with it. Then you give IT a name to tame it, to tackle it and to build up your
tenacity to it.

It's your awareness of IT. It's your acknowledgement of IT. So, you can face IT
rather than duck around the corners and hide from it.

Mine is TURBO.

He's a little stuffed animal dragon that sits on my desk while I work. Dr. Daniel Amen planted the seeds of cute dragons in my mind in his book, *Your Brain is Always Listening.* It's a phenomenal read and I highly recommend it. I resonated with the dragons and simply retained the idea of Naming it to Tame it based off of the theories in his book.

Now, TURBO is super cute. Like a little puppy you just want to keep patting on its head. He's ocean blue with specks of golden glitter with tiny little ears and wide-eyed droopy dog eyes that draw you in with complete awe.

TURBO is a total grade-A cuddler on the outside.

But TURBO on the inside...

Unleashed?

Unsupervised?

Whoa!

Lookout!

He is a fiery combination of all my unresolved fierce feelings totally unsatiable, unstoppable and unreasonable. He jumps to old conclusions, exhausts every emotion, catastrophizing the end of world AND will whip me out from under my feet as he leads me into his lair of lies.

Do NOT let his cuddly looks fool you. He is no Care Bear with positive energy powers pumping from his belly. YET, I made him cute because I found it easier to forgive him. To give him grace and to accept him and his fire breathing flaws just as he is.

TURBO represents my feelings. Right or wrong and in any and every moment when I feel abandoned, rejected, lost, hopeless, confused, frustrated, angry, hurt, dismayed, misunderstood and all those other emotions on the feelings wheel they give you in the counselors' office.

He is everything inside me that attempts to sabotage me. He is everything inside me that projects from my past. He is everything hurt and still healing inside of me. He is my unresolved issues, and he is my hang-ups still waiting for me to habitually repeat.

So, what happened BEFORE Turbo?

How did I understand my unmet needs?

How did I identify what I was feeling?

How did I manage my inner turmoil when it came to surface?

How did I face opposition standing in my way?

And where did all my projectile anger, rage, hurt, frustration, annoyance, disappointment, and sadness go when all my BS rained down upon me?

I didn't and IT didn't.

And IT showed in a flurry of emotional ridiculousness and spiritual warfare on my psyche.

And on others.

Let me tell you about a time when I didn't have TURBO so you can see for yourself.

When I owned my gym, I had a side door that opened to a little green grassy area. The sky was always so blue on that side of the building. The sun would shine bright and hot there, piercing your skin with its warm rays. It was beautiful, it was peaceful, and it was a breathtaking place for me to just be. Yet for some reason,

193

I sat there during what I thought were only crushing end of life moments that stopped my heart and shut me down.

One day, I was going about my business. You know wasting time scrolling on social media. Life wasn't great. But I was managing as I had recently broken up with my boyfriend and business partner (yep same person) at the time.

I was functioning. Barely. But functioning.

As I was numbing out while running my finger up the phone, I was stopped suddenly in my scrolling, like a Mack truck had just hit me. THERE he was with his stupid Facebook post gloating about him and his new peach.

Blah.

Ugh.

My disbelief as I read his caption ignited an immediate civil war in my head and heart.

Disgust

Disappointment

and Disrespect all at once.

The shock was sending every stress signal to my brain lighting a fire inside me that shot my heart rate through the roof and belted out a scream from the depths where I know now TURBO comes from.

On the front line, I was fighting a war within myself, even though I KNEW this was OK.

We were over.

Him and I were done.

Done-done.

And had been done for quite some time.

BUT...

But we had been together for so long and through so much together, how could he?

Already?

So soon?

Seriously?

Did he not EVER really love me?

Was he just throwing it in my face?

WTF?

I'm down here grinding in what used to be our business, trying to pull it up by its bootstraps and there he was up there having ice cream and smooches for lunch.

IT was all running rampant races through my mind sprinting from conclusion to conclusion about how I must NOT have ever been good enough. That I never mattered. And I could not shut it off.

I had a gym to run. I had a business to run, and I had to do it all ALONE. I had 10 classes to teach and bills to pay and kids to go pick up at school. AND all that day.

I was three months behind in rent and had no room for this bullshit that surprise bitched slapped me at 8 o'clock on a Monday morning. So, I went outside that side door and sat on the hot concrete burning my ass and painfully allowing the sun to beat down on me while my mind was in a WTF loop.

I was devastated and could not move.

I was paralyzed in what was.

In the why.

In the how could he.

I was questioning everything.

I mean, e-v-e-r-y-thing.

And it hurt.

It hurt like death hurt.

I sat there for five hours punishing myself in my own mind. True story. No lie.

This strong, independent, tough-love, truth-telling, never-give-up-keep-going-don't-be-a-baby-coach was being just that, a big fat fucking baby.

For five hours, I replayed this bullshit over and over in my mind.

I stared at their picture.

Suffering.

Sitting in filth.

When I finally got the fuck up, I was numb by all the feelings that were in the driver's seat.

I didn't have TURBO to help. I was on my own and I didn't know how to get unstuck.

My legs were numb. And my mind was mush. I was crushed by my own inability to get the fuck up and move.

Maybe five hours doesn't sound like a long time to you. But it was an eternity that day. Especially with the responsibilities I had on my plate.

I never forget that day.

Those feelings.

That shut down.

That break.

I use it to remind myself every time something off setting happens and invites TURBO out to play.

NOW, I give him five minutes to fuck around in the dirt. He can get as filthy as he wants.

He can

Yell

Curse

Cry

Scream

Phone a friend

And act like the world is ending.

TURBO has full-fledged permission to FEEL all the feels. He gets to acknowledge that what is - IS. And like it or not, sitting in it won't change anything except for the time of day.

I got up from the hot concrete after those five hours and moved not just physiologically but MOVED psychologically too. I shut off the social media and told everyone I knew to NOT even as so much breathe the first syllable of his name. I wanted to throw a 50 lb. dumbbell from here to there. I wanted to shatter his world the way he had shattered mine. I was still stuck in his Facebook land long after the five hours had clocked out.

Days passed. Weeks went by and my months grew shorter. Consumed in what was and what should have been according to our original plan. I felt like I was in a time warp of wondering WHY. I felt defeated. Unloved. Unworthy. I felt used up and wasted. I even felt jealous and hungry for his love even though I knew, I KNEW, it was NOT the love that I needed.

Eventually, I managed to MOVE physically because my kids depended on it. My clients expected it. And my core values demanded it. But INSIDE... In my mind ... I was stuck sitting there staring at his and hers smirky smiley selfies.

Blah.

Ugh.

Sigh.

Cry.

Vomit.

So, I learned a trick.

Each day I gave myself time to pity in my pain

Day one: take as much time as you need. Clearly, I used this time up with my five hours in the sun that day.

Day two: I get to do it all over again, BUT I can't let it go on longer than the previous day.

Day three: I found I didn't need that long to release the pain. A few minutes and then POOF! I was good to go.

By day four, my pity party was lessening to a passing afterthought and at the end of the week, I was functioning and up running again at full throttle waving away

WTF and WHY.

Eventually, I didn't need the time to sit in it anymore and promoted myself to what I now call Name It to Tame It and I set TURBO's timer to five minutes anytime I feel the urge of his uprising.

To advance to the next stage, Acceptance, you MUST acknowledge what you are facing.

You have to get a grip on the facts versus the fiction and YOU have to feel all feels.

You won't always need a day or a week to throw baby tantrums. You will eventually master the art of Name It to Tame It, but you can't get to resiliency if you aren't willing to acknowledge and identify the adversity that came for you in the first place.

You MUST Name it to Tame it.

So as soon as you get the eff up and move from it, start asking yourself questions:

How are you feeling?

What are you feeling?

What's the real reason?

Where is this really coming from?

What is fact?

What is fiction?

What is exaggeration?

What is in your control?

What is not?

What would alleviate this feeling right now?

What can I do right now to move from this – right now?

RIGHT NOW.

To make a difference. To rise because of it. And do it out loud.

Yes, you heard me.

Be the crazy person walking down the street talking to yourself. Your brain will start to listen. Then it will start to process and progress.

It sounds ridiculous, but it works. You can even go one step further and go get yourself a TURBO. A figure. A token. A visual reminder. Anything that will help you check yourself, so you don't wreck yourself. He provides a powerful visual stimulation for me that reminds me MY feelings are NOT in control.

I AM.

But go get a new name.

TURBO is taken.

I didn't forget the questions...they are up there behind you – go back and answer them and make friends with your TURBO. He's waiting to help you understand YOU, love YOU, see YOU, feel YOU, and release YOU.

ROBYN MCLEOD THRASHER

A Receiving of What Is

An Awakening to Reality

The Art of Acknowledging Without Settling

A Knowing of Conditions Yet Making

Them Your Own

accepting **acceptance**

there is no amount of coercion, manipulation or 3AM
conversations trying to convince the centers of the
universe otherwise

Take a breath.

Pace yourself.

We,

YOU

Are closer than you think.

Next step is Acceptance.

Now that you are aware of IT. You've named it. You've acknowledged it.

You must now ACCEPT it in order to press on and in through it.

Ugh.

Insert loud unnecessary shoulder shrugging sigh here.

I hear YOU and your hesitant, resistant, rebellious eye-rolling teenager sighs.

BUT LISTEN - it's not as difficult as you think. It's way easier to do than to continue fighting that it happened and that its existence is still taking up space in your mental, emotional, and spiritual capacity making it nearly impossible to move onward and upward, which fucks with your physical capacity to even show up at all.

Accepting doesn't mean you like it.

Condone it.

Or even agree with it.

It's just looking it square in the eye and saying I see you.

Acceptance is receiving something to be true. It's a willingness to take in the unpleasantry. It's saying ok. It is what it is. And I can handle this.

Our hesitation towards acceptance is most likely a twinge of fear combined with the stress of the unknown. And the coupling of the unknowing of "how to" and the toddler/teenager inside of us whining I really don't want to. BUT when we move towards it, in the face of it, welcoming it home, we often discover acceptance is easier than all the anxiety induced uneasy anticipation of it.

Upon my first follow up visit to the doctor after they had removed my spiny dinosaur pieces, I was given a list of my new permanent Cant's.

Yep, That's right.

They were NOW going to TRY to tell ME what I COULD NOT do.

Ha.

Who did they think they were talking to?

I mean, after saving my life and saving my legs, how dare they propose such a thing?!

On the list of NO longer can-do's were:

Roller coasters.

Horseback riding.

Bicycle riding.

Boxing.

And lifting a barbell above my head.

The first three weren't deal breakers for me, but the last two were a HARD HELL NO.

To add fuel to the piss-me-off fire, I was then handed a lengthy list of expectations for my future self. AKA, the long-term aftereffects of an unwanted surgery that saved my life came with bonuses of:

Cold weather causing stiffness

Sitting too long

Standing too much

Lifting heavy objects

Laying on my stomach

Wearing heels

Bending over

All these things would cause MORE pain than I was already in.

WTF?

I guess I would spend the rest of my life moving not too little, but not too much to avoid the potential trigger of exacerbating any additional afflictions.

Long term, I should also expect degenerative bone, muscle and tissue loss. Arthritis and osteoarthritis are most likely too. Plus, the nerve damage and neuropathy would likely feel like fire running through my veins from my back all the down to my toes and probably in both legs and then back up again through my spine to my brain.

WHAT?!

WTF?

WHAT'S THIS BS?!

Has anyone ever even had fire running through their veins because I'd like to meet the beast that can fucking take that shit?

WE, my doctor said, (though I'm pretty sure he meant just me) would also need regular checkups to ensure the deadly infection stayed at bay. He then went on to mention more MRI's and scans and regular blood work for a few months, and then for a few more years in all this BS aftermath.

Just effing great.

Here, I had been naively thinking that when I woke up from anesthesia - the bad dream that was once ruining my life had been taken care of and was eliminated from its existence. WHEN in my new reality it had simply transitioned into a new one that would now have no end.

I went home defeated looking at my new "you can't do list." BUT that machete swinging eight-year-old girl with the dirt under her fingernails came energetically knocking on my door screaming *chop, chop, lets go whack some shit up.*

At each follow-up visit, I persistently asked the same question ten different times, ten different ways.

When could I do this? When could I do that? Could I at least try boxing? I promise I'll just punch the air. And what if the barbell is light? Just the bar. No added weights or plates. I promise. I swear. I'm doing all extra physical therapy. Can't you tell?

Every visit I begged.

I pleaded.

But every passing doctor's visit ultimately ended in me walking out rejected by his definite, definitive, disapproving NO.

My Machete Mentality was made up with the mindset of TOTAL REFUSAL of the finality in his doctor's orders. So, in my defiant, driven and determined there-is-always-a-way mindset, I worked around it.

I pushed limits. I tested the waters. I tried a little. Hurt a lot. I would pull back. Try again. And again. Sometimes it hurt less. Sometimes it hurt more. But I took every green light to push a little bit more.

This sideways way around approach to accepting my new very limited lease on life went on for a year.

Look, I'm the girl that when told NO, squints her brow and says, let's fucking go. I'm the girl that can take the pain of a fishhook lodged in her hand and let her dad pull it out with his bare hands.

I was not going to accept my new script of can't dos.

More than a year of visits went by. More than a year of repeating the same asked and answered questions went by. I wasn't in denial. I was just trying to find A WAY. That little girl in me was dead-set and determined on going back to all her BEFORE old ways.

BEFORE this had happened, I was in the best shape of my life, setting daily PR's and rocking eight-pack abs. BUT, it wasn't until several years later when I was running my gym and coaching 17 hour days that I had finally realized MY version of ACCEPTING was the way I was meant to follow all along SO that it could mature and grow a peace and a place inside of me that God needed me to appreciate and to see.

I had forgotten that I was ALIVE. I had forgotten that I had legs and full use of my brain. I had FORGOTTEN that God let me live. That God WANTED me to live. I had forgotten that I wasn't confined to a wheelchair and that I could pick up my babies and walk around, and even run again. I was so focused on fighting for the old me and my old ways, that I lost sight that the NEW WAY had come to SAVE ME from sinking back into the sinful places I had been so used to living in.

Years later, I've accepted that I can ride a roller coaster BUT just once. Anything more induces a suffering on my spine and IT doesn't deserve that. The risk of breaking my back in two pieces far outweighs a bicycle ride and I have opted to just pet the horse on his head rather than saddle up and trot with him.

Now, the boxing and barbell were a grind to get me to agree to. But after several attempts, I accepted that the unforgiving heavy bag had already been beating me and the pain I endured after the blows was too hefty and too intense, jarring my spine and my back and my hips into what felt like hammers pounding my joints and vices squeezing my bones to death.

Barbells have won the bargaining as well. I've accepted the six-foot Olympic beast is no longer my BFF. I lift it occasionally, but with no added weight on its sides and mostly it sits vertical up against my garage wall. And surprisingly, I am OK with that.

Now.

About four years into my manageable recovery, I finally realized my "can't do" list was NOT just a new list of limits BUT they were actually gifts that have grounded me to the memory of the badass I once was and still am, just in totally different NEW way.

ACCEPTANCE doesn't have to be a grueling grind, like it was for me. It doesn't have to take you as long to get there. In fact, you are in charge of how long it takes you to square off with accepting whatever it is you have been trying to run around.

But I get it.

I was that hardheaded too.

Just remember, the way out is always THROUGH, but meeting acceptance, like it or not, is going to HAVE to happen somewhere along the way if you ever plan on making it through the brush blocking the beautiful view reserved for you.

NO machete can whack away the past.

What IS done IS done.

There is no amount of coercion, manipulation or 3AM conversations trying to convince the centers of the universe otherwise.

So GO get real with yourself.

What is out of your control?

What can YOU control?

What can you change?

What can you let go of?

What can you be open to receiving?

What can you come to terms with?

What new perspective can you shake hands with?

Go make your list and study your NEW. Because the sooner you accept the things you cannot change (thank you Serenity Prayer) the better off you'll be.

ownership

A Responsibility to Bench Your Ego

An Ability to Lead Yourself

The Art of Righting Wrongs

A Knowing of Respecting Your Potential

messy **matters**

my little subconscious self set up shop that
no matter how much I earned or how
hard I worked it would never be enough

She sat there across from us behind her big messy mahogany desk shuffling through all my papers I had so proudly put together. They were all organized into sections with dividers and post-its and paperclips. It was a beautiful work of art, I had thought. She mumbled this and that to her paralegal assistant as they hymned and hawed over the perfectly packaged project that I had presented to her.

My boyfriend had come with me for moral support, but honestly, it was just reinforcement for me to follow through on this fuck up I had to SOMEHOW make come undone.

We sat there together watching them wonder over all my paperwork. We were waiting for direction. For next steps. For a process. For an answer OUT. MY palms were clammy and sweaty as my boyfriend took my hand in his. He looked at me noticing my nerves were a nervous wreck.

Let's take seven steps back.

It's like that moment when you're watching the movie wondering if you missed something, but they just started the scene ahead and had to take you back in time to ensure they've hooked you to sit all the way through the scenes leading you back to the cliffhanging moment of how it will all turn out... well here you go.

One week prior, a strange red car had pulled up to my house. A woman got out of the car and rang our doorbell. My son had been home alone at the time, and he knew not to open the door for anyone, and so she left without a note or inclination as to her purpose that day. He told me about the woman in the red car when I arrived home that evening. Perplexed as to who this could be, I wondered for a few days thinking it was a census surveyor or someone asking me to witness their Jehovah.

BUT, that whisper, it stuck with me in the back of my mind. Trying to figure it out. For some reason, that know-it-all gut of mine was not letting me let it go.

A week later she came calling again, meeting me on my front porch steps and greeting me with three gut wrenching words.

You've been served.

And then five more.

I need you to sign here.

WTF?! TURBO was mumbling inside.

Calm and cool, I took the papers and signed my sloppy signature to accept the envelope with only God knows what was inside.

AS I opened the package, bigger than life, grown up words jumped off the page and out at me.

Lawsuit

Clerk of Court

And a five-figure number with a bunch of names and abbreviations after them.

I had gotten one thing right.

It was God all right.

He was calling me out and up to bat.

Now remember all those credit card bills I didn't pay when I was eating cheesy eggs and trying to keep the electric on and make it paycheck-to-paycheck???

Well... somewhere between being regularly insufficiently funded in my bank account and MY boisterous, bold and badass living-the-American-Dream self, had spoken into existence that ONE DAY I would be debt free...

That I would live in financial freedom, that money would never be a problem again. That I would earn an income that would allow me to impact and influence lives all over the world. That my kids and my love and my family wouldn't worry about funds. That I was on my way to financial abundance as I changed the world by exposing all my screw ups one at a time. That I would be able to answer prayers with my paychecks. That I would be the one answering prayers for help rather than on my knees begging for God to help me.

Make NO mistake, God is ALWAYS listening and apparently had heard enough of endless chatter from me. His patience had grown weary and was ready to see me move on this great financial freedom I had been so fervently speaking about BUT my action taking on it was uneventful and lacking tremendously.

The lady in the red car had been His deliverer challenging me to a game of chicken.

I'll move when you move, He was saying to me.

That day, I finally understood that I would not be granted any further financial means, or responsibility, or freedom from the stress of it all, if I did not shut my mouth and face the fact that nothing would change unless I faced my five figured feat.

Money was something I always struggled with. Growing up, I heard my divorced parents fight easily about money. Child support this and child support that.

Tell her the money is in the mail, he would snidely say.

Ask him why its late again, she'd snicker back.

One dad said it didn't grow on trees and the other said it would never be enough. AND that was some BS I kept telling myself as a virgin entrepreneur, as it had stuck with my childhood ears and limited belief mentality.

My parents gave me everything they could. I wanted for nothing. BUT I also felt their pressure of paycheck-to-paycheck and rested daily with the resentment they had for it. I never learned anything good about money. It was all bad, bad, bad. Too much. Not enough. Running me dry. Tapped out. I've got no more to give. It's always something. What do you want now and how much is it - it seemed?

I got a job at 15 scanning groceries as a Publix cashier. I babysat on the side and learned how to make a dime, value my time and earn independence. In college, I lived solo, worked three jobs and paid most of my own bills. I was blessed enough that my parents paid my college tuition, my car insurance and my mom slipped me a few twenties from time-to-time from her secret stash which when she gave it away - it always seemed like it made her feel free.

I knew WHAT it was to work for a living, for a roof over my head, for fun things and for bills that adulthood brings. But I didn't know how to budget or save or invest or manage the income I was grinding for every single day.

And then it happened one day as I walked across college campus, like love at first sight, hypnotizing and mesmerizing me, I saw the answer to my worries sitting under the sun breaking through old oak trees in the form of the weekly campus vendor market lined with vultures thirsty for signatures for the shirt off your back with their illusive, deceptive credit card applications that gave away money for FREE!

I was given a credit card with a $20,000 limit.

I know, right.

Craziness.

And just like that, at 19 years old, I first found out how simple it was to spend more money than you had AND oh yeah, you didn't *really* have to pay it back.

Within a year of spending, I was the full $20,000 in the hole plus some because they left out the tiny little dirty details about accumulating interest and fees and percentage rates.

When I finally came clean with my hefty secret, I was advised to file bankruptcy. I would never have to go to court to face the music or even pay a penny back. I even got to keep all the things I purchased with it. It simply took the same signature that invited me into the five-figure confinement to also unleash me from its disarray.

TURBO perks up from a sleepy nap and says, *such a well learned lesson, wouldn't you say?*

No one ever taught me otherwise. Not school. Not my folks. My parents had plenty, but never plenty enough. And what enough they did have, they argued habitually about it.

Rich people have money.

Celebrities

Famous people

Doctors and lawyers

They all have money.

Not people like us.

People like us can get Money, but we don't GET to keep THE money.

So, my little subconscious self, set up shop that no matter how much I earned or how hard I worked it would never be enough. Money would forever be a source of turmoil and disagreement with penalties that caused people pain.

So, fast forward back to the Mahogany desk, we sat there waiting expectantly for the answer that this would all be over in 90 days. That I would sign off on the court documents that forgave me and let me off the hook once again without having to pay.

We were shocked when she looked up and said,

I can't help you. You're all over the place. And to be frank, this is a total mess. You need to clean this up before I can even look into maybe possibly filing a payment plan on your behalf, but even then, I don't know.

Wait, WHAT? TURBO perked way up. Both his ears cocked mystified at her righteous rejection.

And that will take months, probably a year if I'm being honest, she said.

Wait, WHAT?

My perfectly placed together bank statements and lists and table of contents were a total mess? I had spent days and hours preparing them.

Did she just say a whole year? Did she just call you a hot mess? TURBO nudged at me announcing his undivided engagement by eavesdropping into our conversation.

Yeah, I think so. I think she just told me I wasn't worth her time. That she didn't see a way.

This perplexed us both as we sat there with my boyfriend in total bewilderment at her blocking our way.

Meanwhile, my man was sitting super calm. Like the best fucking duck on the pond. I think he was waiting for me to lose my shit and was super impressed that I held it together while standing stunned in the parking lot just a few minutes after she had hit us with her denial of handling my financial mess.

You're welcome, TURBO sings proudly for maintaining his composure and not losing his Sh$!

In the parking lot, I turned to my boyfriend and sternly said,

This is God telling me NO. He's telling me to take ownership. That I've got to face it. That I can't write it off, wish it away or pray its redemption and health into existence if I don't lay it all out on the table and become more responsible for it.

He nodded and we got in the car and drove home. Dead set and determined to find another way.

Let me tell you, that little 8-year-old machete making girl came out swinging.

Again.

I went home with the hefty credit report they had printed out for me and the very next day I was on the phone calling the creditors straight down the list. And I HATE the phone. Technology, putting things together, telephone calls and traffic all make TURBO turn over.

But I did it anyway.

I conquered the damn phone and called every single one of those creditors. Even the ones not looking for me. I was put on hold and given number after number after number to call and was transferred from representative to representative a gazillion frustrating times. But, within two weeks, I managed to machete my way into debt negotiations, pay off plans and make final payments closing out accounts and past due collections.

My hot mess was no longer a fire I was trying to escape. In fact, finally taking ownership of it, felt like the sitting down after a long day and taking your shoes off kind of relief.

Whether you like it or not YOU ARE RESPONSIBLE for what you do with your filth EVEN if you aren't responsible for it getting there in the first place.

Now in this case, I was undeniably guilty of complete ownership. I could choose to keep wishing for the financial freedom I was running my mouth about, or I could woman up and listen to God's call to set my sights straight.

If I wanted freedom, I would have to finally face the way I was showing up in it. Which was honestly, no way at all. Once you come to terms with the role you played or are still playing in your mess ups or madness or whatever IT is ness...You can start asking yourself much more powerful questions that will have your inner TURBO shaking in his knees.

What is this teaching me?

What did it come to disrupt?

Where is the opportunity?

Where is the lesson and WTF is it supposed to be teaching me?

What could I have done better?

Where do I need work?

What will I do next time?

Because next time IS COMING and you need to be prepared with a win in your confidence arsenal.

So, ask yourself hard questions and then answer the harder ones.

And machete that shit until you find some answers to help you OWN all your BS.

Where do you need to take ownership in your life right now? What do you keep talking about but doing nothing about? What are you avoiding? Ignoring? Trying to take shortcuts and an easy way out? Are you placing blame? Are you wishing at your vision board or taking action to step into the life you've creatively created on the corkboard in front of you?

ROBYN McLEOD THRASHER

pain

A Bleeding in Your Heart

An Enduring of Unhealing Hurt

The Art of Experiencing Love and Loss

A Knowing of Grace

inner **owl**

he is perched high above
the chaos below
contemplating a calmer
way out

We've covered

Awareness

Acknowledgment

Identifying

Accepting

And owning...

Now, the question is HOW do we reason all of that out in our day-to-day?

A great counselor of mine once shared with me the psychology behind our brain's capacity to process what's going on around us and within us.

First, he explained there is our **Logical or Reasonable Mind** saying Oh my Lord, Stop, Wait, Yes, No, What if this, What if that, I should be doing this, or hold up now I'm frozen in that, even though I know it's not fact.

AND then, there is our hopeless romantic, idealizing, over-rationalizing, dramatic, chaotic, spitfire, spunky, toddler tantrum throwing, rebellious teenager, catastrophizing end of the world this our last chance **Emotional Mindset**.

Those two alone can get us into a whole new level of **Stuck & Settled** and weave an even bigger mess in our lives rather than just in our heads. We ensue in a tug-of-war with our own voices yanking us back and forth until one voice crosses the line temporarily winning over our mindset and leaving us in less powerful state beaten down by the back and forth that outlasted our ability to endure the banter of them both.

The KEY to winning is tucked away somewhere in the middle of the two, ducking punches, swatting lies and maneuvering self-serving logistics. It's our **Wise Mind** sitting all chill and cross-legged meditating while the other two duke out their best Oscar winning performances again and again and again.

Now our Wise Mind is a combination of what we know to be true (our logical mind) and our emotional mind (think TURBO), which is what we reactively and impulsively do.

This combo, I call our **Inner Owl**. *I can't help but to think of the Tootsie Pop Owl here, but you go with whatever image you see.*

He is perched high above the chaos below contemplating a calmer way out. It's our gut saying go. It's our instincts kicking in and saying no. It's our wisdom waiting for a hi, hello, and yes please help us, we are in need of your expert mindfulness, patient ease and calm demeanor that does not react or respond but SEES.

When I was fuming about the ex and his peach, my emotional brain was on pedal to the metal in the driver seat, while my logical mind knew I should not care, but nonetheless was stuck in the backseat buckled in tightly bracing for the impact that was coming for me. They were both corroding all the space in my brain that could decipher a crystal-clear picture of relief for me.

Meanwhile, my inner Owl was watching me waver back and forth and in between.

It was muted with its big round eyes just staring at me hoping I would ask him to intervene, but I didn't know how to engage him for a cease fire between the facts in my mind and my heart on fire from all my crushed dreams.

Accepting what once was and what NOW IS takes a good, hard, long look in the mirror at yourself while asking all the hard questions I've given to you to contemplate and ponder in HOPES that you can break free.

Now, I'm going to be a little B here and say MOST of YOU will NOT do the work.

You'll highlight and underline and read through, but you won't do the work and you'll leave the last page of this book and then you'll HURRY back to your being stuck.

Engaging your inner Owl to spread his wings is like listening to someone say I told you so, setting your ego aside and looking up in agreement. It's a humbling practice that can and WILL bring you inner peace. It's the splash of cold water you need in your face, subduing yourself in knowing, when your overthinking gets the best of you and your TURBO takes the rest of you. Meanwhile, you're left frozen in your feelings with no real way to distinguish mindfulness between the two and your inner Owl is pacing in circles waddling and waiting to awaken you.

And when you do WAKE UP - you're still Stuck. Trapped in what was or never will be again. You're alive, but not living. You're still abandoning the life inside. Letting the SCREAM go on and on and on as you long for the previous version of you that was familiar and felt wayyyyyyy easier to fall back into.

So how do we tap into our inner Owl? Engage our wise mind? Become more peaceful, even keeled and insightful?

You ready?

Here it comes.

.

.

.

Start by doing all the shit in this book.

Yep.

That's it.

Answer the hard questions.

IN the fucking mirror.

With your eyes WIDE open.

Face Your Giants.

It's arguably my most valuable core tenant and principal in life that gets the most voice in my personal and professional life.

FACE YOUR GIANTS.

Monthly

Weekly

Daily

Hourly if you have too.

But FACE them.

Ask yourself the questions you're avoiding because of the BEFORES.

Ask yourself the questions to become more aware of their existence.

Ask yourself the hard questions to acknowledge their presence, but without providing them any additional power over you.

Answer the questions that make you want to shy away.

Answer the questions that will help you lead your life in a taking ownership - without losing my shit - kind of way.

Ask them Out Loud

Ask them Vulnerable

Ask them Honest

Ask them Real & Raw.

AND then, END the cycle of the runaround around them.

It's pretty effing hard to lie to yourself in the mirror because your eyes already know the truth. They'll look back at you and say, NOT NOW mother#*$#!!

And then channel your best of Benson & Stabler SVU and continue to interrogate the hell out of yourself without a break.

Face. *Insert clapping hands emoji here.*

Your. *And here.*

Giants. *And one more for a melodramatic effect, here.*

.

.

.

Now breathe.

.

.

.

Cause I know you're already back in TURBO state pushing away all those unwanted, overwhelming feelings and thinking I'll just throw myself back into work, or wine, or chocolate, or chips, or chips and chocolate and wine.

Stop That!

It's going to take you a minute.

In fact, it might take you awhile.

And that is OK.

And you might not like it.

And you know what, you don't have to.

You just have to acknowledge it.

Admit it.

Accept it.

You don't even have to fully understand it right now. That will come later.

YOU just have to pick up your machete and start whacking at it.

You don't need another perspective, or doctor, or plan, or book, or one last Google search.

The answers you're seeking are all already inside you.

You don't need another day or month or year to adjust or let it all sink in.

IT'S IN.

It's sunk.

That's why you're so fucking stuck and have settled yourself so effing deep in it.

What YOU NEED - IS to release it.

AND there is no other way than where???

That's right.

Through IT.

And we are going to get through IT by Facing IT.

The only thing you need RIGHT NOW in order to start tapping into your inner Owl and gain ground on your BS is to know that **Everything you need is already inside you.**

Everything.

God has given it to you. It's just underneath all your filth from BEFORE. And another news flash, He doesn't care about the dirt on your back. He knows about ALL that too. He knew the adversity coming for you. He knew the level at which you would rise into your resilience or NOT. He knows your inner TURBO and don't forget He gave life to that SCREAM inside.

You're just NOT listening.

Or doing.

Or believing.

Or all the above.

I didn't have to like that he moved on without me. But when I accepted it, I realized I didn't like it BECAUSE he beat me to the punch and got to move on first. It wasn't because I still loved him or wanted him back. It was because I didn't MOVE for me.

I didn't like the lawyer lady telling me I was a hot mess. But when I owned it, I learned I actually liked cleaning up my mess with my own Carolina Mountain machete.

I didn't like losing my home and living in my gym. But when I asked my inner

Owl which way to move, he pointed in the direction of my dreams and so I did.

Letting my house and materialistic items all go in HOPES of a bigger purpose I had heard from listening to the screaming shouting from deep within.

It took me nearly seven years to Face my Giants and get them all out.

Seven years of standing in front of the mirror, breaking eye contact to blankly stare down at my thin, little, pale aging hands.

Seven years of looking up and down and away at ANY mirror that came to greet me on the wall.

Seven years of HOW could you? WHY did you? You're NOT. You CAN'T.

And a whole lot of Why? Why? Why? WTF?

Seven years of tears.

Seven years of red eyes and a splotchy face.

Seven years of snot dripping off my cheeks and dropping to my knees mostly on my cold hard bathroom floor.

Seven years of crying quietly in the shower praying the water would drown my gasps for relief from my retaliating in believing I was, in fact, already FREE.

Seven years of trying to simply say I FORGIVE YOU and it's OK.

Seven YEARS.

Until finally, looking up one day, and seeing that the face in the mirror had finally surrendered all her fears and all her plans and all her BEFORES, freeing up the space to release each and every scream that was long overdue to be freed from its suffering.

So DON'T wait.

And don't take seven years to manage your mindset. YOUR inner Owl IS there.

Perched patiently and waiting to guide you to freedom.

When do you recognize your inner Owl is at work versus TURBO or vice versa? What situations ignite your logical mind and send you into a fact checking overthinking planning preparing loophole? What can you do to start taming your emotional mindset? Cooling off your fiery fight a tad bit rather than letting it burn without a thermostat?

What Giants are YOU NOT facing? Which ones are holding you back? Which ones are YOU stubbornly refusing to wash off? AND what will HAVE to happen in order for you to raise your head and Face the Giants looking back?

adapt

A Feeling of Flow

An Ability to be Flexible in Your Feelings

The Art of Shifting Through Storms

A Knowing of Your Capacity to Adjust Acceptingly

lanky legs

i was determined to learn
my new way around and
there would be no further
resistance on my end

We are so programmed to stay with what we know. With what's easy and familiar. With what's safe and comfortable. That no matter how much we claim to want better, WE keep chasing the same thing(s) over and over and over again.

Hello... Seven years...

It shows up differently in different spaces of our heart, challenging our thoughts, actions, and beliefs, BUT make no mistake, we chase what we know is familiar even if that familiar is a foe...UNLESS we adapt and learn the lessons hidden in it.

Adapting sometimes shows up disguised as uncomfortable and awkward. So, we show up thinking we look silly, embarrassed, and humbled by our inability to do so seamlessly. We're much like a baby giraffe wandering around with lanky legs for the first time, fumbling and stumbling in an open field, drunk on determination to stand tall with our new feet.

Adaptation is where WE, YOU, ME - all learn to live again, but differently. And hopefully, BETTER, I believe. Adapting will demand your patience to tame your TURBO and then require your dexterity to maneuver the wheel quickly away from your feelings as they fight to drive your life in reverse here.

AND they usually do it all together and all at once. Teaming up against you and the progress you're making through all of this somewhat normalized life happens adversity.

Adapting will require an insatiable hunger that gives ALL its undivided attention to the NEW life rather than fighting for the same old beat-up BEFORE one.

When I was learning to walk again, I was forced into adaptation. FORCED. This thing had happened to me, and my legs said SO WHAT. As did my back and hips and my pissed off resentful heart.

But the quicker I adapted, the faster I could go forward from the medical constraints working against me. The quicker I could start again.

So how did I adapt? I busted my ass at PT.

I followed my physical therapist's rulebook. I asked for extra reps. I took my time to NOT be a dumbass and hurry it all along, BUT I always did a PLUS ONE of everything and anything I could get my hands on and I pushed ahead with my baby giraffe feet hoping eventually I would get used to my new life by pouring tons of energy into overcoming any pain that persisted against me.

I remember the first time my physical therapist suggested I go back to the gym and perform my PT there. A friendly and familiar scenery. Might cheer you up, he said as he shrugged his shoulders, smiled, and smirked. BUT what I really saw was his eyes say,

Here's your chance to show up in your very own Rocky-like way. You've taken the hit. Now, get the F-up because you're not the type of girl that takes a blow and doesn't come brawling back.

So, all excited with anticipation, I hobbled my way into the gym with my saran wrapped PICC line still several feet threaded in and underneath my skin. I made a bee line for the stretching mats, kneeled and took a deep breath before beginning bird dogs on a gigantic Swiss ball that would in theory hold me up as I built the strength back up in my scrawny skinny lanky new legs.

With my belly against the ball, my head down and one arm and opposite leg outstretched to make the lift, all I could muster out was a silent ugly cry. My hair fell to cover my tears as I squinted up my face - frozen in a frustrated state. I was crying and feeling sorry for myself in my own pity.

It made absolutely no sense. At therapy, I was a rockstar. The favorite patient banging out reps and asking for more while everyone else complained and gave half-ass effort into their assignment to fix whatever ailment they had. But here, at what was once my home away from home, my refuge from the reality I was secretly living, I just watched everyone around me running and lifting and sweating and talking and rushing past me like I was the slowest car in the fast lane.

I wiped my face, got my shit and left without doing one single PT exercise.

The overwhelming emotions of not being able to do what I could always do - in a place where I was the badass mama that everyone wanted to talk to - was profoundly paralyzing. I realized, confined at therapy, I was on the top of my game. I was coming back changed, corrected and in a way being perfected into my NEW life that was preparing me for the paths of the purpose He had in mind for me.

BUT back at my old stomping grounds, I wasn't at the top of my game. I could only window shop the Zumba and Les Mills Combat classes. I couldn't be on stage or in the front row killing it to every beat. I couldn't front squat and hang clean my bodyweight much less throw wall balls in between. Hell, I was sweating from just getting up off the floor and walking in the door.

It was depressing.

And I was mad.

Mad this happened. Mad I had to start from scratch. Mad that everything I had worked for was for nothing. Mad that I had notebooks and notebooks of workouts and PR's that had just been wiped completely clean. Mad that my muscles were mush and there was not one shred of evidence of my past kickass repeat performances that I had accomplished so many times before.

My BEFORE had left the building. It was long gone, left in an operating room and thrown in with the hazardous waste.

I wish I could tell you something poignant. That I had this great epiphany that night lying in bed. But I don't think I did. I'm pretty sure I was just sad, sitting in my suffering.

But I think I needed to feel it then.

The suffering.

The settling.

The sitting in it.

Literally getting stuck in my own body - as my back and my legs and my hips tensed up in what felt like a bone crushing vice, squeezing out the old life fighting to grow back inside of me.

It was like the five hours I lost that day at the gym when I saw him with her. But much worse. It was like the second I heard the words, *She's Gone*, knowing I would never get to hear her voice again. But much more miserably worse. It was like the picking and choosing what "things" to leave behind when I saw the eviction notice. But much more shamefully painful.

The next day I went back to the gym and tried again with my skinny, wobbly and weak little giraffe legs. Still sullen and wallowing in my own pity, but I was determined to win back even the tiniest smallest piece of my dignity.

Nobody noticed.

Nobody cared.

Not one person.

But I DID.

That day I stayed at the gym for a long while. I was determined to learn my new way around and there would be no further resistance on my end. I would ADAPT to what was given to me. And LET GO OF what I used to be.

So, I did my bird-dogs and side-lying leg lifts and held onto the wall for balance as I tried to bend over performing one-legged deadlifts. It wasn't pretty, BUT I showed up ugly and I showed up adapting and accepting and acknowledging and owning that I WOULD have to force myself to meet this NEW version of the machete whacking fishhook me.

That this new version was designed to be better. That she would suffer less in the end if she showed up NOW. That she would live alive with purpose and a mission to walk taller somehow even though in those first few moments she couldn't see but one foot ahead of her past defeats.

And being defeated was WAY worse than those one-legged deadlifts.

So I bent over and balanced on one lanky leg until I touched the floor, rose up, stood tall and bent right back over to do it all over again.

Adversity gives us all kinds of gifts. But I think the best one is learning we have two lives to LIVE and YOU GET TO PICK which one stays and which one you get to evict.

So, what's your adaptability rate? Do you adapt? Can you? Will you? Are you hanging on to the past? To the remnants of what was? How can you become more flexible and accepting to a different version of your life IF you were to LET GO of your BEFORES and BS? Is there anything anchoring you to the resistance of adaptation? How can you have a fresh perspective on an old BEFORE, so that you can redirect your energy to the NEW you waiting for YOU to get unstuck from settling?

Are you willing to suffer short-term while you figure out a new way or would you rather be defeated for the long haul waking up in the nightmare of what used to be?

resourceful

A Grit that Gets the Job Done

An Embodiment of Creative Genes

The Art of Crafting Any Which Way Through

A Knowing of Can Do Will Do Must Do

move like macgyver

the clock is ticking and the longer you stare
the faster time ticks away

It's 1985 and MacGyver was the man.

My brother and I sat up late nights watching his stealth like performance as he performed perfectly under extreme pressure.

Something was almost always about to blow up while he and several other people were locked in a small room somewhere in the middle of nowhere and HELP was never on the way.

We sat there on pins and needles, edging closer and closer to the TV screen, biting our nails and mindlessly cramming kernels of Orville Redenbacher's movie theater butter popcorn into our mouth while sipping a fizzy orange soda or diet coke.

Would he make it out alive?

Would they all survive?

There's just no way...

Gasp!

How will he ever get out of this one all OK?

And then SUDDENLY, our minds were blown away, as he narrowly escaped the explosion or the fire or the flood or whatever crazy crap the writers had intended for his potential demise.

And we just couldn't believe it!

THAT he always got out alive. And always just in the nick of time without one second to spare! It was a miraculous moment that charged the adrenaline in our veins.

In my eyes, MacGyver, was a machete-that-shit superhero!

Now, I already told YOU, you already have everything you need inside. Everything. God didn't leave ONE thing out. You just have to start thinking differently. Like MacGyver.

So, let's take a deeper look at this guy that glued us to the TV and mesmerized us with his machete mentality masteries.

First of all, MacGyver was

Resourceful

Calm

Steady under pressure

He made shit happen

He saw a forward path where others saw a cul-de-sac

He saw solutions

Possibilities

And HE made a way out.

Typically, with rope and matches and paperclips and happenstance objects strategically placed for his purpose, BUT he got out. He saved the sticky situation. He accomplished the impossible. He functioned under fire.

So how do we learn from this 80s television character who is arguably the only man on the planet that could make a mullet look sexy?

Simple.

Seek Solutions.

When the door is locked, the Machete Mentality says rip it off. Remember, there is always way.

If the door has hinges, you can take them off and walk right out or walk right in, you just have to flip your focus from the problem to seeking solutions to solve them.

There are NO problems.

Only Possibilities.

For instance, have you ever called your friend to vent?

Of course, you have.

And what did you vent about?

Yep!

That's right!

The problem.

Duh!

BUT what you should have done instead, WAS brainstorm solutions. You wasted perfectly good minutes on repeating a problem, complaining about a problem and blaming a problem rather than seeking solutions and finding a way THROUGH the problem.

MacGyver didn't spend 45 minutes talking about the problem. He shut up and got to work. He sought solutions and stepped up. When the others froze to be doomed, he led the way through, which ultimately meant out.

Now I get it,

I hear you.

You're thinking I don't have much to work with.

MacGyver had a TV crew and a perfectly laid out plan prepared for him by producers and writers. But Seek AND I swear YE shall find.

Everything you need, you already have. The books on the shelf you haven't read. The ideas in your head that you're dreaming about. Could be something as simple as starting with a walk around the block or picking up pen and paper and journaling what you're feeling flooded with.

I promise. It's already in YOU. Or you wouldn't be reading this book this far - STILL.

So, WRITE this one down,

Do what you can, with what you have, with where you are, right now!

I'll wait.

Go ahead.

Do what you can, with what you have, with where you are, right now!

Doesn't matter how many black clouds you've got floating around. Doesn't matter how old you are, how broke or tired or beat up you feel. You CAN do something to START something with what you have right now.

But the doctor said...

But when I was in college, I tore this and that...

But my parents this...

But I've been...

But my kids...

But my other half...

But the bills are piling up and I don't...

But I don't know how...

Fuck that shit.

Start.

Now.

Remember, there is an URGENCY to YOUR life - NOT just everybody else's.

Do what you can, with what you have, with where you are, right now!

Right now.

I repeated this again and again to my clients at the gym. As we ran the clock down with burpees and box jumps and rope slams, I reminded them second by second with every drop of sweat:

Do what you can, with what you have, with where you are, right now!

And THAT is the simple key to moving like MacGyver.

I mean check it...

Imagine if MacGyver gave all his energy to looking at the bomb.

Just looking at it.

He's standing there all rugged and manly with his sandy brown mullet with crossed arms laying on his chest. His bottom lip pursed and his eyebrows are raised. He says, looks like we got a problem, huh? And then continues to stand there and stare. Or gossip. Or vent. Or whine. Or complain.

Come on.

Seriously?!

What if that were the TV Show?

Go ahead.

Laugh out loud.

It's ridiculous!!

We would be screaming bloody murder at the TV for him to move.

To act

To do something

To try anything

We would be outraged by his immobility.

So, the next time you're fixed on the assumed finality of some problem, imagine yourself just standing there staring at it like a bomb. The clock is ticking and the longer you stare, the faster time ticks away. The camera zooms in on the fuse as its sparks are running down the wick quicker and quicker and quicker.

You would do something.

You WOULD.

You would fight for your life to the bitter end.

Well guess what buttercup?

This IS your life.

And the END shouldn't be bitter.

But back here in real reality TV land, YOU aren't doing shit. You're staring at the bomb. Waiting for its explosion on your life.

So go yell at yourself in the mirror, but this time stand there and say:

Do Something

Do Something

Do Something

GO fucking DO something!!!

Anything but stand there staying stuck and sinking and settling into your BS and BEFORES. MacGyver isn't coming to save you AND neither is anyone else. But you can certainly step up and save yourself by seeking solutions. I guarantee you there is always a way AND you will ALWAYS see it just in the nick of time if you give to HIM and you look within.

So...

BE resourceful. Get creative. Take initiative. Think proactively. Search high and low, all around you and within you. It's there. Just slow down and breathe. It's right there inside you waiting for you to open your eyes in the wonderment of just how really simple it is.

PUT down the complaining and resentment and guilt and shame and hopelessness and desperation for the nothingness that is in your BS.

Seek solutions. Seek strength. Seek striving. Seek Success. Seek a salvation in knowing there is nothing else you need to get unstuck, to make miracles out of your messes and to take ownership of the FACT that YOU are totally in charge of saving yourself.

Move like MacGyver. Quit waiting on him.

What are your awesome traits? Your badass skills that you KNOW you possess? Are you the friend that complains or the friend that suggests solutions? Do you cheer people on or are you the leader stepping up, taking charge and leading the way? Are you first to volunteer or do you shy away? What character traits do you love most about yourself? Are you figuring out ways to save yourself or waiting on someone else to show up and take over the reins?

courage

A Fierce Faith Filled Decision

An Unsteady Step into Uncertainty

The Art of Doing it Anyway

A Knowing of Needing to Know

becoming **bulletproof**

it teaches you to quickly catch glimpses of your past
movie-like life conflicts, choices, challenges, and all
the changes you've previously been though

Moving like MacGyver will get you out…BUT you're going to
need some protection from the rapid-fire life is waiting to shoot out at you like
daggers the minute you do, so it's time to armor up.

For me, that means wearing a bracelet around my wrist to remind me what
promise I've made to myself on any given day. Think Wonder Woman's gold cuffs.

Pray Continually.

Do it Anyways.

Be Fierce.

God is within her; she will not fail.

Those are just a few sayings etched in each of my bracelet's engravings. Sometimes,
it's just having TURBO sit and stare at me while I work and write that suits me up
for a productive, kick-ass, devil can't distract or derail me kind of day.

OR it's my post-it promises I have everywhere (yep literally everywhere) with
quotes and verses that pull me back into a courageous confidence for when I catch

the devil sneaking into MY moments as he tries to make a move towards me.

And my favorite, of course, are my leg warmers and cardigan like capes. Somehow, they make me feel suited up just like Wonder Woman ready to defend my day.

These tangible things help me prepare. They help me produce. They help me defend. They help me win. And they help me make the best choices I can to keep me moving ahead. They set the stage for me. They set my pace. They suit me up for facing anything that the devil wants me to think I can NOT accept or adapt to with the right mindset.

Becoming Bulletproof is all about wearing your armor in the name of utilizing the advantages that come from winning over your adversity.

Now, you are more than welcome to allow the pain

the hurt

the difficulty

the trauma

the hardship

the whatever IT is to GET YOU

OR

You can let it GROW YOU.

Choose Your Own Adventure, right?

I know it doesn't seem like it sometimes, but YOU ARE, very much in total and complete charge of YOU. How you handle you, how you respond to you, how you fight for you OR how you do nothing at all for you.

It's a Get Up or Stay Stuck Mentality. Taking us right back to choosing our choices and owning that where you are today is a direct result of a choice or choices you have made or have failed to act upon because you thought hoping they would eventually just go away.

Like it or not, YOU ARE, the sum of all your choices added up and equaling to this very day. All the turns you took. The lefts instead of rights and the rights instead of wrongs. Even NOT making a choice, is a choice. Decision fatigue sets in and is a big fat B if you let it win.

Becoming Bulletproof is going to heavily rely on your instincts to call upon all those past hurts and discover patterns that pulled you here today HOPING for some kind of direction or help. You'll have to keep questioning yourself, not to torture your scars or drum up old BS, but to develop a new awareness about yourself that will have you believing the choices you made don't have to define you any longer.

Own it.

Being Bulletproof isn't a full-blown immunity for when adversity hits again, but it does aid in your victory, preparing you for the rapid machine gun fire heading your way. It can and will equip you physically with little visual reminders like I've mentioned above, as well as getting you on deck mentally, posturing you with an inside power that can prevail immediately under any unwanted pressure.

It teaches you to quickly catch GLIMPSES of your past movie-like life conflicts, choices, challenges, and all the changes you've previously been though. Allowing you to borrow your courage and confidence and clarity from what once was and USE it to now lead you THROUGH your new oh-my-God, how-to, what now, here we go again, decision making blues.

Glimpses of your past life linger. Either letting the light in or leaving you longing to feel them all over again. Like the chorus of your favorite song, you can repeat them over and over without looking at the lyrics. They are on repeat in your head and have a permanent home in your heart.

Come take a little glimpse with me.

.

.

.

See a woman living a picture-perfect Pottery Barn style life

See her sick and pregnant and scared to death wondering what if

See a woman climb into the backseat of the black car he pulled up in

See a man painting her toenails and combing her hair

See them laughing and smiling, sneaking in seconds of secret time together

See him put on her socks and walk her steadily up and down the corridors when she is frail

See her through the sliding glass doors hooked up to machines and monitors feeding her multiple medicines and waiting for them to heal her

See her laughing and smiling and playing with her kids too enveloped by their innocence to be worried by what they didn't find in all the tests

See her walking to the altar and dropping to her knees

See her greet them, cheer them, and encourage them while her heart breaks silently beneath all the atta boys and Yays for their fitness journeys

See her win the trophy and cross the finish line in spite of the pain ripping through her veins

See a woman screaming out loud, bent over kneeling in her own despise, crying out for a sign from Him that the fire burning her soul won't take her alive and away from them

See a woman being pushed up against a wall by a strong forearm

See his elbow in her face, the spit on her cheek and the red marks left after the forced embrace

See a woman throw a wine glass and run out in a rage

See her speaking before a crowd urging them to fight their fight and never give up their relentless race

See her go from doctor to doctor to doctor sitting in a worried wait

See her laying on a dying woman's lap holding on to her brittle hands just a little too tight

See her make the decision to not have the baby and then sit on Sundays in silent shame

See a little girl playing in the mountains and brushing off all her machete whacking filthy ways

See her standing up at Sunday school class reciting all the right verses for an accolade from memorizing rather than relating

See a little girl race her bicycle across a greenway as she cuts across the golf course searching for her brother only to find him smoking cigarettes at just 13

See her hide in her bedroom crying and heartbroken from seeing his first disobedience that would lead to his many falls from grace

See her raise her hands in utter defeat, throwing the good book in the fire as the flames light up and burn its heaviness into ashes, dust and then to her shame

See her fade into black with an empty absence yearning for so much more as she gets back into the black car and rides away with her demons deconstructing every last little piece of her.

.

.

.

I think your glimpses give you clues to what you're seeking or missing or longing for. They leave hints of patterns and habits and actions and reactions. They serve as steppingstones for growing as you skip along in life like a rock on a creek that bounces and bounces and bounces until it sinks beneath.

My glimpses crave LOVE. Importance. Priority. A first-place finish. They reveal a once wandering lost little girl in a woman's body searching for a home where she is adored and treasured without any insecurities and shadows of second-best leftovers, hold-ups because you're not on fire-fires.

What do your glimpses give away of you?

Can you glance back at them? And then stand boldly in your past and present-day truths?

Can you see yourself surviving all of them?

Steven Furtick preached a phenomenal sermon called *Greenlight at the Red Sea*.

10000% you should YouTube this regardless of your beliefs, religion, or hardheaded that ain't for me mindset. It's packed with life-changing perspectives that will shift your memories and put your dreams into drive.

The turning point takeaway is when Steven yells

When You Don't Remember, You Rebel.

Boom!

Mic Drop!!

And a very loud Hallelujah!!!

When I was listening to him preach, I was excitedly wailing out loud many multiple Yes! Yes! Yeses! Accompanied with my hands clapping in rhythm with his perfectly pitched prophesizing. IT was the entire essence of my bulletproof mentality.

When you don't remember, you rebel.

So how do you remember so you don't rebel and go down the rabbit hole projecting an imaginary hell?

Well, YOU start with the glimpses.

So go back and go there first.

Yep, right now.

Then ask yourself the questions below. And yes, preferably face-to-face in that bathroom mirror meeting you've been putting off.

List all your struggles.

List all your wins.

List all your lies.

List all your truths.

And start connecting the dots.

Don't forget those glimpses.

Those defining moments.

Those U-turns.

Those pivoting points of redirection that took you through a choose your own adventure you did not expect.

.

.

.

What did you overcome?

What was transformed inside of you?

What was transformed in your environment?

In your mindset?

In your heartaches and heartbreaks?

What can you remember?

What did you forget?

Did you forgive yourself?

Or are you still holding a grudge?

Do you need to forgive them?

Do you need to forgive you?

And where did you get all that gumption to GRIT your way through it all?

What did you do?

What was done to you?

What did you wish you didn't do?

Can you walk away and leave it all behind now?

Can you do it again, but better?

And are you REALY giving it your all?

How have you reacted in the past?

How did you handle it?

How can you handle it now?

Where you are in life?

And where do you think you should be?

What's keeping you from being there?

And don't say YOU – that's too surface level easy.

Who were you then?

Who are you now?

WHO do you NEVER want to be again?

If you can reintroduce yourself to that crazy-good, amazing human staring back at you in the mirror, you'll see the 8, 9, 10-year-old kid you once were. You'll see the child inside with all the dreams and wishes and unjaded missions is still there trying to break through all the filth you have failed to clean up since then.

If you can recall all the good you've already done, you can retire the rebellion against your future self that deserves a helping hand right now.

Being Bulletproof is a fierceness you walk into your history with and bring forth the highlight reel of every single battle you've ever fought, whether you won or lost.

It is doing IT anyway, and in spite of...

Well, you fill in the blank.

In spite of, _____, I will move anyways.

In spite of, _____, I will keep going.

In spite of, _____, I will keep my promises I've made to myself.

In spite of, _____, I will remember how far I've come.

In spite of, _____, I know I will prevail once again.

In spite of, _____, I will remember and not rebel.

That's Bulletproof.

It is remembering all your past hits and getting up faster because of them. It is taming your TURBO in 5 minutes AND it is not staying in survival mode OR sitting in the suffering of it. It is not wishing to go back to all your BEFORES and have a love affair with your BS.

Bulletproof is taking responsibility for what you did or didn't do. It is your inner Owl showing up to the party & holding your car keys while the MacGyver in you is on the move being resourceful seeking solutions in a matchstick moment that you so desperately do not want to go up in flames.

Bulletproof is catching glimpses of your old movie-like life and then generously giving them the gift of grace. It is knowing the difference between when you need a break and when you need to brace yourself for that right gut punch quickly coming to steal your breath and beat you from experiencing the freedom in fighting for your future self.

It is asking the questions. Especially the ones you've been foregoing in hopes they would forget your name. It is choosing where your attention goes and trashing anything else your mind tries to savor in self-sabotage mode.

Being Bulletproof is asking is this **Helping ME** or is this **Hurting ME**? It is one of my most favorite post-it promises I have stuck to the inside of my head.

Is this action I'm doing helping me or hurting me? Is this choice I'm choosing helping? Or is this choice I'm choosing hurting me?

Ask yourself

At every decision

With every choice

Wherever you're at

Again

and

Again

And

Again.

Is what I am doing or about to do – **helping me or hurting me?**

Anything that isn't contributing to helping you, crumble that thought up and trash it. Anything that isn't a step forward forging towards your most magical movie-like ending, machete that shit and forge on without it.

It really IS that simple.

Try it. Put it on a post-it and make it your promise to yourself *(and while you are at it, be on the lookout for YES, another book "The Post-it Promise" releasing in 2023).*

Bulletproof is reminding yourself THAT you are more than a survivor.

You are a fighter. A pioneer. A leader. A soldier. A Carolina Mountain fortress forger. A Wonder Woman, a Rocky or a MacGyver with a badass brilliant inner Owl all wrapped up into one.

So put on your armor and start swinging your machete on the way up and on the way out.

You saw all those questions back there...go on, get after it.

again

A Second Chance

An Ability to See Beyond the Period

The Art of Reflecting to Refine Actions

A Knowing that the End is a Spiral

Without One

always one **more everything**

you keep going until God pulls you aside
and says well done

This one is easy.

Always do more.

If you think you should.

You Should.

If you think you can.

You Can.

The fact that you are asking the question, Can I do more? Means absolutely, **YES**, you fucking can.

Sometimes, it just takes one more day

one more rep

one more mile

one more email

one more phone call

one more conversation

one more full-hearted attempt

AND YOUR LIFE can be totally transformed.

So, YES, GO DO ONE MORE.

I hated those questions when I was a trainer.

How many more should I do? How do I know if I am doing enough? Is this too heavy or should I go lighter?

As a trainer, I know I'm the one putting together the plan, but remember, I don't care much for numbers and statistics. I don't care how it works. Just THAT it works. And the only way to know for sure that it works is to get your hands knee deep dirty in the DOING of it.

I care that it's ugly before your allotted time to be done is up.

I care that you grunt and curse and fall to your knees and that you are breathless and on the verge of losing your breakfast. I care that you finished past the buzzer and gave it one last rep.

I care that you did better than last time and that you showed up with the intention to give better than your best.

I care that when you're done, you are done. AND that You don't have one ounce left. The tank is empty. And that you gave it 10000000000000000000000000000 00.99 fucking percent.

So, when my clients asked me, how much more?

I lied.

Every single effing time.

Three more

One more

Ten more seconds

Just a little bit longer

Last song

I never knew based on a number because My ONE MORE was to push them past the predetermined limits, they had set for themselves upon walking into my gym. My goal was to obliterate any objections, limited beliefs and lingering laziness that resided inside their souls.

My ONE MORE was pulling out of them the potential they had long-ago put-on pause.

My ONE MORE was going to drive them into defeating their disbeliefs.

My ONE MORE was going to go one more until the energy in the room said NOW we are done.

Now, for those of you who love legit science studies and research about the phenomenon of how long we can "go" if we knew we were eventually going to be rescued, here's a little story about rats that will leave you in amazement.

There was this test called the Hope Experiment back in the 1950's. Dr. Curt Richter conducted a study out of Harvard University to see how long rats would actually tread water before giving up. The rats were placed in water and left to swim or tread. The first test was about 15 minutes in duration before the rat's showed signs of fatigue and started to sink. They pulled the rats out dried them off and let them rest for a few minutes before sending them back to the tanks to start swimming again.

Do you know how long they lasted the second round?

Five minutes?

Ten minutes?

Thirty minutes?

Nope.

It was a phenomenal sixty hours.

Yes.

I said 6-0 hours!

They lasted up to 60 hours. Holy what Wow! Are you kidding me?

My first instinct was to say, I couldn't swim for 60 hours.

BUT I bet I could if my life depended on it.

If I knew rescue was coming, I would keep treading and keep my head above surface however long it took.

And the rats knew. They had an expectation that they would be rescued. So, they kept swimming or treading or believing. Waiting 60 hours to eventually be freed. They were brought through before...therefore, they would be brought through again.

So, they kept on keeping on.

They didn't give up.

And thankfully so.

I hear you saying it's not that simple.

BUT YES, actually IT is.

You've just never gone long enough to see.

You've given up too soon.

You've cut corners.

AND bounced around from excuse to excuse to excuse. You don't keep on keeping on long enough. You don't do MORE than necessary. You let yourself sink beneath at the first sign of weariness that holds you down and you FORGET you actually have a CHOICE to CHOOSE.

Sink or Swim.

I mean.

A rat did it.

Why not you?

So go do MORE for as long as it takes.

One more degree

One more second

One more minute

One more hour

One more day

One more month

You keep going until God pulls you aside and says WELL DONE.

If you knew with that 10000000000000000.99% certainty, that YOU would be rescued

That YOU would win

That YOU would get relief on the other side of all your pain

That everything you have been through and up against would cease to exist

If you just went one more anything -

YOU would keep going.

You would do just ONE MORE of whatever it took.

To the very next day

To the very next moment

To the very next ALL IN one more good machete whack

You would NOT stop swinging until there was nothing left to whack.

Just think... that ONE MORE you've been tucking away, saving for a rainy day, might be the one more that releases everything existing inside of you that saves you from tirelessly treading in the same stuck and suffering old second-best place.

The question is not CAN YOU do one more? But WILL you do one more? Will you go beyond where it's easy and normal and natural? Will you push your limits? Test the waters? Do what is forced and challenging until you become compelled to show up differently and rescue your own damn self? Can you recognize where in your life you call it quits just one too little? One too short? Why do you think that is? AND can you see what a difference ONE MORE will make? Are you willing to tread 60 hours with an urgent endurance to save the life suffocating inside you?

love

A Fire Burning Inside Your Heart

An Indestructible Choice

The Art of Giving Without Want

A Knowing Worth Suffering For

ROBYN MCLEOD THRASHER

what's the point

at the end of each day, it couldn't
outlast my urgent enduring
patience to stay the course I had
created for me

When life has its grip on you and you're at your lowest low, it's going to be hard to go one more. It's going to be hard to ask and answer all these questions. It's going to be hard to keep going. It's going to be hard to rise up. It's going to be hard to be bigger than your Goliath inside. It's going to feel bigger and stronger and braver than you could ever be.

BUT the hard of it all - IS what ultimately makes you.

Believing otherwise is just another lie we slip into telling ourselves.

You're going to want to quit. To give in. To give up. To hide. To run. To isolate with TURBO and forget that you've got your Owl to steer you into smoother waters that don't keep continuously crashing above and over and on your head.

You won't always have to tread water.

It won't always take giraffe legs and 60 endless hours.

BUT on many occasions, you will feel like What's the Point?

Again

And again

And again

And again.

You'll get lost. And tired. And lonely. And confused. And discombobulated in the middle of all your messes. You'll work and work and work only to get knocked down again. You'll see growth and get excited that THIS is IT! Then you'll see nothing. For days and weeks and months and maybe even years.

But hopefully not seven.

You'll wonder What's the Point and be tempted to fill that void with things that hijack your healing and sometimes even your humanity. You'll wonder What's the Point and start to slow your pace. You'll wonder What's the Point and contemplate changing lanes, turning around and searching for an easier way.

Wonder.

But don't waver.

And don't wander too far.

Remember, the only way out is THROUGH. And sometimes, asking What's the Point, is the only question that will lead us there.

What's the Point gives us back our awareness to our choices. Our acknowledgment of the circumstances standing there, but NOW knowing those circumstances do NOT have to dictate our next one more.

What's the Point reveals our ability to adapt and to endure and to evaluate the BS, the BEFORES and the Screams refusing to be silenced into settling.

What's the Point forces you, us, me to address and question ourselves on what we are filling up with. Because if it's the wrong filling, well, we will falter on our follow through and won't have the right fuel to fight for the next best version of you.

Throughout my journey, I can't count all the many What's the Points I almost fell victim to. So many days were wasted, so many nights were worried, YET waking up each new day I was un-jilted and ready to go for it all over again.

I chose to focus NOT very long on the What's the Point with a bad attitude. I chose NOT to let What's the Point get the best of me. We battled for sure. We went through decision fatigue and delayed plenty of good moments and momentum because What's the Point put up some pretty good effing points.

But at the end of each day, it couldn't outlast my urgent enduring patience to stay the course I had created for me. There was a path for me only I could machete and braving my What's the Point was just another brush I would have to whack out of my way.

Living this life I love, free from my BS and BEFORES and walking hand-in-hand with my Screams – was, is, always the Point for me.

Finding this freedom was the fix I needed. Not the lies and let downs, not the TURBO running unleashed, none of that compared to the feeling of accomplishment of knowing and understanding and forgiving and accepting and embracing the ME I was - while I was becoming ME.

Your What's the Point will be different from mine and from others. BUT, the only point that matters, is the one you are searching for and fighting for and ultimately living for.

And along the journey, well, sometimes we do things that don't make sense because What's the Point gets us, wears us down and breaks us OR it can fuel us to fight furiously and fast for the future you, we, all need.

Our choices usually start off with good intentions and high hopes, while onlookers snare at us with judgments that can absurdly throw us off course. SO always remember, this is YOUR trip. It doesn't have to make sense to them. What's the Point ONLY has to resonate with you. Make sense to you. AND at that time in your life because it might transform along the journey WITH you.

What's the Point only has to fill YOU up with that patient peace and that urgent enduring that equips you to get up each new day and be right with yourself. And with God.

For me, my What's the Point, is LOVE.

Love for Myself.

Love for Him.

Love for My Kids. And Love for their future, free of generational blocks and burdens that I am overcoming for them.

Love for my self-worth and integrity.

And Love for my future husband and marriage that I vow a faithfulness and honor in.

Love for My Dreams. That they get to live out loud, wild and free.

Love for MY Wishes.

Love for MY Deep-Down Screams.

Love for My Future Self. AND Love for all my past BS and BEFORES that I pray I'll never see again.

So Whatever IT is for you…Whatever YOUR What's the Point is… choose your choice of living for the good side of it. Because it IS there if you choose the choice to step into it.

Because **What's the Point of Resiliency**, when you're down and out and your wounds are dug open wide? Well, I think it's YOU walking taller with an energy and an attitude of unstoppable intention for the things that you know are meant to be ONLY yours. For the things waiting on you. For your resolve to NOT settle, to NOT suffer and to NOT let yourself sit second best to the shadows that sneak up on you and try to dim your light.

Because **What's the Point of Adversity** - when you're hurt and crying and grieving and shedding crushed dreams and broken promises? I think you already know it's the second chance of learning the lesson again, except finally surrendering it all to Him, then getting back up and doing it all over again, but better.

Because **What's the Point of NOT Settling or Staying Stuck** when it's easier to live in shortcuts and in the comfortability of an acceptable worldly complacency that begs us to live in a standard normalized watered-down version of what our lives could have been? To effing experience all there is. To fall asleep on your deathbed peacefully full of stories and adventures and heartaches that made us and gave us a life legacy that we actually lived in.

Because **What's the Point of Endurance** - when you are tired and weary and worn and defeated and can't see past the desert dryness that has become your life? I KNOW, I know it's to keep trusting and believing that if you keep going, if you keep dreaming, you'll outlast the fleeting feelings that follow you around slowing you down and eventually, eventually, eventually you'll make it to the point past all the painful weighing down and find your freedom waving you in.

Because **What's the Point of Facing Your Giants** – when they keep coming for you fervently? Easy. To Find Your Freedom. To Live Relentlessly. And to be Authentically Awake, Alive and Living out your Dreams.

For me, that's cursing and still loving Jesus all at the same time. That's meeting myself daily at the mirror AS I AM and LOVING every broken bent bruised bold brave badass piece of me. That's showing up ugly for my future self again and again and again, hopefully just a little bit better each day I get to breathe another breath in.

For me, that's Never Giving Up on the Thing I believe most in - LOVE.

A Simple. Truthful. Honest. Enduring Love that Never Leaves Me.

What's the Point is that I want you to remember The Machete Mentality when you're in the quicksand of your pits sinking slowly and choosing choices that are enticing you to quit.

1. **GET** the F@$! **Up**. Pull yourself up physically and psychologically and powerfully from anything that implores you to stay down. Fiercely fight it. Don't get caught outside in the sun soaking up your sadness.

2. Know your **TURBO**. Slap an identifier on anything that lights the wildfire in your worry. And then pause just long enough to understand, acknowledge, accept, own and adapt from it, and to it, and with it, as it fuels your energy to fulfill your responsibilities to your Screams stuck down inside of you.

3. Invite your **OWL** to lead the way. Give him permission to referee your overthinking dramatic ways that try to take over the reins.

4. And do what you can with what you have with where you are RIGHT NOW. **MACGYVER** it. Don't stare at the bomb until the fuse is about to give. Save yourself by finding your answers within.

5. **ARMOR UP**. Put on vivid visuals of yourself winning again, breathing again, enduring again. Play your highest highlight reel again and again and again until it plays out like your favorite movie you never want to end.

6. And then just keep going - **ONE MORE** day. Give it all you can. Then give it again. The key to your deliverance is determined by your willingness to believe that there is nothing, no Goliath so grand, no path too overgrown, no mountain so steep, that you can't machete your way through it even if it means getting stained filthy along the way.

different

A Unique Version of Similar Things

An Outlet to Color the World

The Art of Setting Yourself Apart

A Knowing in Permitting Permission

To Be Undeniably You

you **don't**

i watched them suffer and satisfy themselves with staying put because the pain of their pain was just too much

As I write these last few pages, I am in excruciating pain. My head is pounding, and it feels like daggers are piercing my brain. I look over at my love driving me home from a week working in the A-T-L and find solace in his Rising Phoenix tattoo inked on his right arm. I don't know what it is about his tattoo. It's just a place of comfort for me. It soothes me when I see it peeking out from underneath his sleeve. Like it's saying, Hey I'm here. I got you.

Meanwhile, inside my head, TURBO is silently wailing over every WEB MD explanation of the hardening headaches that have been perplexing me for the past three weeks.

What if it's a brain tumor? I say out loud to my other half.

People get brain tumors all the time, you know.

He looked straight ahead at the highway and simply spoke,

People do...

Then he quickly took his blue eyes off the road, glancing at me, smiling and firmly said,

YOU Don't.

That's it right there! The Machete Mentality. Summed up in two words.

YOU DON'T.

It's THAT shift in perspective that we all need to carry and conceal.

YOU don't settle.

YOU don't suffer.

YOU don't give up.

When life happens and settles against you

YOU make a way

YOU go through

YOU endure

YOU remember

YOU overcome

YOU rise into your resilience

YOU listen to the screams

YOU live alive

YOU set yourself free!

Quietly, I repeated his words so TURBO could hear me and feel me easing his fears about the headaches wearing us down to our knees.

YOU Don't.

I smiled and went back to typing these glimpses of me in hopes that someone, YOU, will pick up their machete and start whacking the hell out of their old, used, washed-up BS and BEFORES.

I did not choose Resilience to be my thing

But it is.

And I am grateful for it choosing me.

It came to me from choosing all MY choose your own adventure choices. All the opportunities done, and all the opportunities undone, abandoned, alone, untouched and left lingering in the unknown. My resilience was birthed from moments of crying and begging and pleading and bargaining and borrowing, emerging from a place inside of me that was too hungry to settle for seconds, too stubborn to stay suffering in my own shortcomings, and too hopeful to sell out the life living inside.

I grew up watching the people around me settle, get stuck AND stay that way. I watched them make choices that made me scream and die a little on the inside. I watched them suffer and satisfy themselves with staying put because the pain of their pain was just too much.

The fighter in me has resigned my anger to this. TURBO doesn't get pissed off anymore at their blind eye to a better life living inside, because through it all I have come to accept, I cannot change anyone else's own mentality, BUT I CAN keep fighting for my own.

So, when everyone else Gives Up

Says Stop or No

I'm that girl moving in the pain

in the grief

in the heartache

in the sickness

and in the sorrow and in the loneliness of it all.

I'm the girl with resilience and endurance and finding a way in my blood. I thank my Pa. I thank my God. I thank every sickness, every sadness and every suckiness that pitched a tent in my path. They didn't expect me and my machete to show up swinging so strongly at all their wicked ways.

I know right now you might feel so very far away that you can barely hear the shallow cries of the scream inside. I know right now you might not feel like you have the stamina to paddle your head above for another 60 hours. That you're not so sure you can be all MacGyver-ish and machete your way through all the BS. I know you're questioning the simplicity and want to intercede with complicated instructions worrying and overthinking and analyzing everything. I know your BEFORE is gripping you in a stronghold and your energy is running on empty to be able to break free from settling in it. BUT that's the side of you rebelling now, shushing your inner Owl and letting your TURBO take you down.

I don't have all the answers. I'm just 45 starting out on this journey I've pulled out of me.

My authority isn't in science or research or psychology or any type of theology for sure. It's in THE DOING I have done plenty of. It is in my own memories which I have given glimpses of. It's in my years of experience – Experiencing. And it's in the roar I have from reminding myself I've gotten back up after every single failure, fall after fall.

It's in my courage to release from BEFORE and to fight for a better - I spent the past 45 years treading water for. It's in my mindfulness of knowing I can do just one more. It's in my choices I've acknowledged, accepted, and owned. AND it's in the adapting to the adversities in the messy madness of it all.

It's in my finding of my freedom in the pain of letting it all go, BUT it's mostly, in my God and His mercy for me.

If you get nothing else from this book, promise me this: When the pressure rises, Move. When it pursues you, Move. AND when shallow waters crash over your head, go deeper where you WILL HAVE to tread.

I'll leave you with this one last choose your own adventure story.

Choice #1

Life is happening all around you and TO you as YOU let it. You can sit back and watch the time tick away. You can stay there stuck, settling and sinking into the safest place to be left undone. It is, after all, the most secure space for living life in an uncomfortable complacency without worry or fear of being truly seen.

OR

Choice #2

You can let life happen WITH you, sitting shotgun with the windows rolled down and the radio turned up. Singing out loud, obnoxiously happy and free with TURBO buckled in the backseat with all your BEFORES and BS, while you drive hurriedly steadfast home to the life that has set you free.

Now, most people will WANT to choose choice #2. To live life as I put it, Relentlessly and Alive. Unfortunately, that's not where most end up. Inadvertently, they will get stuck in all the in-between messiness and Choice #1 ends up choosing a paved-out path that circles them around and around and around and never truly breaking free.

But not you.

YOU Don't.

authenticity

A Peace in Your Heart

An Unapologetic Choice to Live Alive

The Art of Facing Your Giants

A Knowing in the Mirror that Smiles Back

just **filthy**

i was stuck and settling further
into the sinking hole that snuck
up snatching me

My brothers and I played in those mountains for years. We believed in the magical lands we were macheting where we won every battle and fought every fight with great valor.

We got filthy dirty for the cause. We got banged up and beat up and squealed when every little big black beetle bug looking thing was trying to distract us from our adventures beyond the uncharted terrain over our heads in our own North Carolina backyard.

We worked endlessly creating our world beyond the woods. Determined to clear new ways up the mountain, to the creeks where waterfalls fell in awe of our relentless ethics for this life inside our heads. We worked in faith. Child-like and certain. That we would stand there and wipe our hands on our pants and tuck our hair behind our ears nodding our heads in approval at the clearing we had created with our own little hands.

All we had suffered for. The cuts on our hands. The sweat in our eyes. The bug bites, the dirt, the red clay stuck in our shoes and stained our pants. The scratches from the branches. The bruises from the falls. The dried blood lines trickling down our legs to our feet, staining our socks and shoes. We didn't care. In fact, we didn't even feel the pain in it at all.

In my mind I see us now, as we just stood there on our new mountain top, holding our machetes to the heavens like Moses' sturdy staff that gave power to his unbelief.

We stood there, where there was once nothing but bushes and greens and lots of tall trees, looking down at all the land we had cleared.

We had arrived.

Achieved the dream.

Checked the box.

Built the fortress.

Brought our own imaginations to life.

We were living it out.

Finally.

And at last.

Interrupted in our admiration, we heard our mom call for dinnertime. So, we turned around together and started our slow descent unaware of how high we had actually climbed. The steep path, while now paved from all our macheting ways, pulled us quickly downwards and forward, causing me to stumble off course. My sneaker easily sunk into the soft dirt. I was stuck and settling further into the sinking hole that snuck up snatching me.

But with my machete in hand, I struck the ground and lodged it into the solid strong path WE had made. And with one push, I pulled myself up and onto firmer land.

My brothers didn't stop moving, they only glanced back to make sure I was good. Nodding and knowing their little sister could figure out what to do. After all, we were pioneers of finding a way - to make our way through.

When we got to the bottom, our mom was somehow widely surprised.

Look at y'all! You're filthy. From head to toe. Just filthy.

She cried out at our dirty disheveled appearance shaking her head and surrendering to our inability to stay away from the off beaten paths.

My brothers and I snickered and smirked and smiled. We knew the dirt she so desperately wanted to Ivory soap off of us IS what led us to conquer our mountain and create a way for someone, anyone, maybe, hopefully, possibly YOU to experience all the goodness that we had macheted through.

She slammed the bar of Ivory soap on the window ledge once again and then stammered off back inside and into the kitchen mumbling words of motherly advice we had failed to heed.

Looking at the white block, we knew what to do.

And as we began scrubbing the filth from our skin, we excitedly planned out our tomorrow and how we would start whacking again.

This Ending is YOUR Beginning.

It's Where You Make Your Machete.

Choose Your Next New Adventure.

And Get a Little Filthy.

p.s.

There is Always a Battle.
Face it.

There is Always a Choice.
Choose Resilience.

There is Always Pain.
Feel it. Endure it. Release it.

There is Always a Way.
Find it. Make it. Live it.

ROBYN MCLEOD THRASHER

thank yous

Thank you **God**, for choosing me. I praise you in all my messes and thank you for all my miracles. I know even in all my unconventional creative gotta-make-it-happen-machete ways, it is YOUR divine intervention that faithfully steps in with perfect timing to make all things work for the Good.

Sam and Dylan, you BOTH give me more strength and power and fullness than my heart can hold. On the days I don't want to get up, You both remind me WHY I do it anyways. I overflow with unconditional love for you and am always in AWE of you. I know I am paving the path for you to do greater things than I ever can or will. You are both SO much more than I could have ever imagined. You are my heart and the best thing I will have ever created in this lifetime.

Thank you to my forever love. Thank you for challenging me, calling me out on my BS, supporting me and loving me as I am. YOU are my rock in this world. My calm. My center. My peace that I can hug. I know God gave me You walking through my gym doors to show me HOW to save myself from myself. You have helped untangle the worst parts of me allowing me to unravel into a perfectly imperfect version of what I was always meant to become. No other love could ever

FILL my Heart and My Life with the Peace and Joy and Laughter that You Do. You make me Better AND I love you endlessly, **Dale Tanner**.

Thank you to my parents who gave me the bones to build a great life. Having four parents made me stronger, braver, wiser, and I am proud to be a little bit of each of you. I hope I have made you proud. I was never trying to break free from the life you gave me. Just always had to go about it in my own way. To **Robin**, my angel in heaven, I feel you in the wind. I see you in the animals. I hear you in every Stevie song. And I toast you over every glass of merlot. To my **Second Dad**, without fail you fixed every broken thing. You showed me how to climb and You taught me that even in the heavy midst of the winds against my face, that no amount of my determination would ever be in vain as long as I gave my efforts to God and went forth in His name. Thanks for always applauding me even when you didn't agree. To my **Mom**, thank you for showing me how to chase my dreams by sacrificing yours. I am the architect you never were just with words rather than buildings. I don't think I'd be living as alive and as relentlessly if you hadn't chosen to live unselfishly for your family. AND to my **Dad**, you showed me what it was to keep my head up. To buckle down and do the work. To grind. To go when everyone else would give up. You believe in me and my crazy dreams as if they were as normal as the sun shinning and the waves crashing at my favorite beach.

Thank you, **Eliza Passardi**, for helping me make this and many other projects along the way. For being the first one to JUMP, to live relentless and to live alive. For all the texts, all the vents, all the long days and all the hard conversations that made us both better. Thank you for taking this relentless walk with me. You are my right hand everything.

To **Vanessa Withers**, my off the wall tell it like it is friend who I have trusted with my heart from day one. You never left my side during all my wrong turns and me choosing choices that made no sense. Thanks for sticking by me and being my sounding board that always knew exactly what I needed and when. But mostly, thank you for buying in and helping make my mission a living reality.

To all my friends and family – whatever role you played in my life, know this, I have remembered. I don't ever forget what you've done for me previously. I hold and carry what each of you have given me every day. In my words. In my dreams. And in my Screams. **Deanee Miller**, thanks for sitting at the backroom table with me. My love for our friendship goes beyond measure for your unending belief and support.

To all my coaches, mentors, counselors, managers, bosses and leaders from my past and present - HOLY THANKS. I've had the privilege of learning from so many amazing people in so many different ways. Mike Finer. Bryan Tobias. Bobby Aldridge. Alex Hormozi. Robert Thompson. Steve Hopper. Anthony Trucks. David Hudson. My favorite teacher, **Ms. J**, thanks for recruiting me and believing in me at such a young age. I carry your teachings as a lifelong support system in my heart every day.

To all my clients - Past and present. Thank you for trusting me as your guide on your journey through everything.

To my readers - The mere fact that you are still here tells me you are seeking something more from the inside of you. So, I pray my words set your Scream free. AND You Live Relentlessly Alive and Free.

Peace Out.

I'll see you on the inside in Dancing with Tsunamis.

Love,

Robyn

dancing with tsunamis

The Waves that Wash Us Clean

Please enjoy an excerpt from
Robyn McLeod Thrasher's
next book releasing spring 2023

waves

A Harrowing Unexpected Experience

An Ability to Move Through
Without Hesitation

The Art of Ceaseless Swelling
in Your Emotions

A Knowing of Sinking and
Swimming Unanimously

the boy who unleashed me

I didn't know I was capable of so much anger and rage.

It burned through me like a California wildfire with distinct levels of heat that hurt and healed me all at the same time.

Desire.

Passion.

Pain.

Chemistry.

Love.

Lust.

Fantasy.

Escape.

It was the kind of heat that envelopes you with its glowing embers, encapsulating you and burning you at the stake of your core.

Within the fire, was a spiritual soul connecting depth I had never known before.

A meeting only God could bring.

And then...

there was the meeting of our demons.

Not skeletons we sheepishly hide until they are forced out of us.

But hardcore demons.

Skeletons you can talk about.

Skeletons YOU can get over, get through, and get past.

But demons...they don't go anywhere.

And the meeting of ours stayed steadfast, strong, and steady in their feeding on one other.

A meeting only our darkest secrets, memories, mistakes, traumas, and regretful hurts caused by our own insecurities, screwups and berating of our own psyches could bring.

God help us. Is what I should have been praying.

I can see myself standing in his way.

Facing him head on. Both my arms stretched out with my hands bracing the bathroom door as if my 5'2-inch self could hold way to his power.

I did this multiple times during our rages.

It was my go-to.

I was the fighter, and he was the stonewaller on lockdown.

I would fight.

Even when I wanted him to go.

My demon fought for his to stay.

His power over me was such a stronghold.

Emotional.

Mental.

Spiritual.

Physical.

It was determined and dedicated to holding me right in the midst of all my own self-induced rage.

And he in mine.

It's that side of you no one knows. That side of you that you didn't even know existed until faced with the need to hold on.

Like fingertips gripping on the edge of a lifeboat, digging in deep as the waters pull you backward, swirling around you as the waves crash over your head. You fight to stay above the surface.

And in the dark of night, THIS is the side of you that you hide from the world. That ONLY you and IT witness.

In these moments, when my fear turned to rage, he could remain calm.

He was cool. And the cooler he was, the crazier I got.

We rarely were ever in rage together. It was a yin and yang, push and pull tornado twisting the life out of the both of us.

I would either stand there begging and pleading for him to talk. To open up. To speak. To stay. To let go. To fight. Or I would be slurring toxic words of hate and anger and at the same time still desiring and pathetically needing and pleading for him to stay.

I needed him to change his mind. I needed him to see me as his only way. I needed him to need me as much as I needed him. I needed him to fight for me. I needed him to fill with just as much rage as I.

To be as lost as I.

To be as scared as I.

And he was.

BUT he just bottled it up inside, corked it tight and let it boil until he burst.

We mirrored each other.

No ones rage was deeper than the other.

It wasn't a competition of who was more fucked up. It wasn't a battle of right vs wrong. We were equally fucked up. And we were equally fighting wars that had nothing to do with each other. But we used each other as punching bags and sounding boards and a place of refuge and relief.

The release I got from him wanting me, desiring me, and using me was undeniably that same hot shower my brother explained as the crack filling up in his veins soothed him... that same rush of hot water was imaginably running down my head, over my body and scolding me from the outside in.

Every time we fought and made up and repeated the cycle again and again and again was a gratification I craved from this world.

AND he so freely gave to me.

He was my drug.

And I was beyond addicted.

Our worlds were intertwined. They collided HARD and there wasn't anyone around to pick up our pieces or pull us apart. So, we stayed at our crash site. And tried to build a life on top of painful rubble scattered with rage and regrets.

It worked for a while. And in my head, it still works. It will always work in my head. This stupid dream of mine. That he could rescue me from death, from grief, from divorce, from crushed dreams, from a broken home, from a celebrity-ish life in a small town where everyone knew our names and the allure of our togetherness was so taboo it lit the fire that much more fiercely.

He was the first thing that made me feel alive in the fog of emptiness that I had been living. Smiling all day and every day for everyone but myself.

But when I was with him, I was alive.

He made me want to grow.

He made me want more for myself.

He made me feel hungry.

And he fed me excitement and passion and chemistry and emotions running wild that I had suppressed for years.

EVEN with the boy in the black car.

THIS was different.

This was real.

This was cathartic.

This was possible.

This was going to be the one who found my soul, saved me and brought me back from living lies.

This was the boy that unleashed me.

This was the boy that would steal my soul and force me to see who I really was meant to be.

And I soon found out, that the ugly inside of her (inside of me) wasn't someone I wanted to be.

The demon would demolish every single one of my fairy tale delusional dreams that this was somehow a meeting of two lost souls.

That because we were saved together one Sunday morning on picture perfect day in southern Georgia, we were connected souls that would surrender our sins to His way and live happily ever after.

But those were figments of unseen fairy tales that would never become the bedtime stories I had been whispering myself to sleep with night after night.

The spiraling winds our demons conjured up to capture us, blew boastfully around us, torturing our every hope, our every desire, our every wish.

We died a little more each day.

Together.

Slowly fading from the celebrity couple I created in my mind to a nothingness that scared the living shit out of me.

Follow Robyn on social media @robynthrashercoaching for updates on the release of her memoir Dancing with Tsunamis. Expected Spring 2023.

a*bout the* **author**

ROBYN McLeod THRASHER is the mom of two kick-ass kids and lives in Tampa, Florida. She is an author, motivational speaker, coach and founder of Robyn Thrasher Fitness, a Transformation Coaching Business that has helped thousands of people change their lives from the inside out.

The Machete Mentality is her debut book, released as a prequel to her tell all, Dancing with Tsunamis, which links together all the pieces from The Machete Mentality. Dancing with Tsunamis is expected to release in early 2023. Robyn is also completing a third book, The Post-it-Promise, which will launch in 2023 as well.

She is a child of God, loves the beach, talks to animals on her morning walks and loves traveling with her second chance family.

To Book Robyn to Speak at one of your events, please contact:

robyn@robynthrasher.com

For more information on Robyn Thrasher and to follow her weekly blogs please visit:

www.robynthrasher.com

You can also follow her on social media **@robynthrashercoaching**

coming **soon**

By Robyn McLeod Thrasher

Dancing with Tsunamis

The Post-It-Promise

Filling Gaps

Made in the USA
Columbia, SC
08 April 2023

15091774R00205